S0-AAE-759

THE USBORNE BOOK OF
WORLD RELIGIONS

Susan Meredith

Consultants:
Dr Vivienne Baumfield and Wendy Dossett

Designed by Linda Penny

Illustrated by Nicholas Hewetson
Map illustrations by Jeremy Gower

Edited by Cheryl Evans

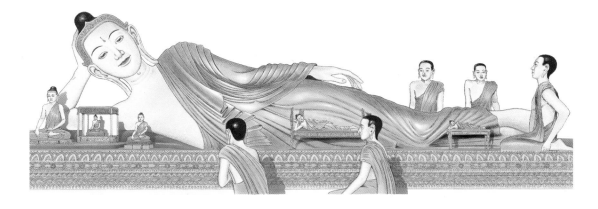

Additional consultants: Bharatiya Vidya Bhavan (Institute of Indian Culture), The Board of Deputies of British Jews, Indriyesha Das, Dr Anne Millard, The Muslim Educational Trust, Rabbi Danny Rich, Narendra and Ila Shah, Annabel Shilson-Thomas, Indajit Singh.

CONTENTS

Acknowledgements
The publishers are grateful to the following organizations for permission to reproduce their material or to use it as artists' reference:

Ancient Art and Architecture Collection, 18 (and artist's reference for festival at Western Wall), 20 (and artist's reference for Isaiah mosaic), 31, 54 (artist's reference for Willendorf Venus and Fall of Phaethon), 55 (left).
Circa Photo Library, 7 (artist's reference for Hindu children dancing), 10 (bottom right), 20 (artist's reference for Holocaust sculpture), 22 (and artist's reference for Ten Commandments carving), 33, 36, 50 (right), 59.
Bruce Coleman, 29 (bottom).
Sonia Halliday Photographs, 30, 32 (artist's reference for Winchester Bible).

Michael Holford Photographs, 11, 14 (top), 25, 29 (top), 32.
The Hutchison Library, 6 (bottom), 8 (artist's reference for devil masks), 17, 35, 37, 38/39 (top), 45 (top), 47 (top), 48, 49, 50 (left), 55 (right).
Lifefile Photographic Library, 16 (and artist's reference for Hindu temple), 29 (artist's reference for pagoda).
Muslim Aid, 9.
Christine Osborne Pictures, 6 (top), 7, 10 (artist's reference for Hindu dancers).
Ann & Bury Peerless, 4, 12, 14 (bottom), 24/25 (artist's reference for reclining Buddha), 45 (right, and artist's reference for Guru Nanak), 47 (bottom).
Peter Sanders Photography, 10 (bottom left), 39 (bottom), 40/41 (and artist's reference for vase), 42, 43.
Zefa, 23, 41 (artist's reference for mosque).

Every effort has been made to trace the copyright holders of material in this book. If any rights have been omitted, the publishers offer their apologies and will rectify this in any subsequent editions following notification.

First published in 1995 by Usborne Publishing Ltd., 83-85 Saffron Hill, London EC1N 8RT, England.

Copyright © 1995 Usborne Publishing Ltd. The name Usborne and the devices ♀ ♁ are Trade Marks of Usborne Publishing Ltd. All rights reserved. No part of this publication may be reproduced, stored in a retrieval system or transmitted in any form or by any means, electronic, mechanical, photocopying, recording or otherwise, without the prior permission of the publisher.

First published in America in March 1996. Printed in Spain.

INTRODUCTION

This book describes most of the major religions in the world, as well as some less well-known ones. It cannot be comprehensive, as there are far too many religions for that.

Even within the same religion, beliefs and opinions vary; this book aims to explain the key ideas in as balanced and objective a way as possible.

The major religions

The six most major religions are generally considered to be Hinduism, Judaism, Buddhism, Christianity, Islam and Sikhism. This is because they have the largest numbers of followers and are practiced in many parts of the world, not just in the areas where they originated. These religions are dealt with in some detail, in date order.

How many followers?

Estimating the numbers of followers of religions is tricky. Some people refuse to enter their religion on official forms, believing it to be a private matter; others may enter the religion of their country or their parents, even though they do not actually practice it themselves. In some places, such as China and Japan, many people follow more than one religion. Sometimes religions compete for members, with religious officials overestimating the number of members of their own faith. For these reasons, membership figures given in this book can only be approximate.

Geography and religion

Some of the differences which exist in religion are partly to do with where people happen to live. In this book, traditions which have more to do with geography than with religion have not been dealt with. For example, the custom of arranged marriages (where a person's marriage partner is chosen for them by their parents) is generally something which has grown up in certain societies rather than having been prescribed by religions.

Calendars

In 1582 a revised calendar was introduced in some Christian countries of the West by the Pope, Gregory XIII. This Gregorian calendar is now used all over the world in business and administration, as well as in the Christian Church.

However, other religions use different calendars for their worship and festivals. Most of these are lunar; that is, they are based on the length of time it takes the moon to orbit the earth. As this does not coincide with Gregorian calendar months, it means that the dates of festivals shift slightly from year to year. The Gregorian calendar is solar: based on the time it takes the earth to go round the sun, and the dates of Christian festivals stay the same every year. The festival of Easter is an exception and is set according to the moon.

Dates and abbreviations

You will be used to seeing the abbreviations BC and AD with dates. BC stands for Before Christ and AD stands for *Anno Domini* (the Year of the Lord). These terms only apply to Christianity. Sometimes different designations, BCE and CE, are used because they are not based on any one religion. BCE and CE stand for Before the Common Era and Common Era.

Dates in the BC period are counted backward from the year 0, so that the 6th century BC refers to the years between 599 and 500BC. The 6th century AD refers to the years from 500 to 599AD.

Where you see a date without BC or AD after it, you can assume that it is AD. AD has only been included in places where it may be unclear without it whether the date is BC or AD.

The period known as the Middle Ages is generally taken to be from about 1000 to 1500AD.

Some dates begin with the abbreviation "c". This stands for *circa*, which is Latin for "about". Historians are often uncertain of exact dates in early religious history.

Pronunciation

A good dictionary will show you how to pronounce the more difficult words in this book. You may also come across different spellings of some words.

WHAT IS RELIGION?

What exactly is religion and why is it a part of so many people's lives? Throughout history and across the world there have been people who believe that something exists beyond the physical world that they experience through their senses.

This girl is using all her five senses, although she may not consciously be aware of it.

Even when you are thinking, or feeling emotions, you are using your brain, which is part of the physical world.

Religious people believe that their lives are given meaning and purpose by something extra. They believe that this something is just as real as the physical world; in fact, it is sometimes referred to as ultimate or absolute reality by those who believe that it is even more real than the physical world.

The spiritual dimension

This other reality is a spiritual, not a physical, one. It is difficult to talk about because it lies beyond what can be known in the usual way, for example scientific facts.

Religious people would say that although the idea of the spirit cannot really be described, its presence can be felt. It is what gives something its innermost essence and distinctive character. In ancient times the spirit was often described as the spark or breath which gave life.

Anything which helps people get closer to the spiritual world is said to be sacred or holy and is treated with great respect.

Carvings on poles like this are sacred to native North Americans. They represent guardian animals, known as totems.

Finding a definition

In some languages, for example, the Indian languages, for a long time there was no such word as religion. Religion was so much a part of everyday life that a special word was not needed for it.

Today, it is hard to come up with a definition of the word religion which everyone finds acceptable. Nevertheless, there are some ideas which many religions have in common.

A supreme power

Religion usually, though not always, involves revering or worshiping a higher, unseen power which is thought to have created the world and now oversees it. This higher power is sometimes referred to as the Absolute. In some religions it is seen as an impersonal force. In others it is more of a personal force, often called God, to which people can appeal for help and guidance. Some religions have several gods.

Most religions teach that the supreme power is beyond description and so they do not have pictures of it. Jews do not even say the name of their God aloud because it is so holy, and it is written in an abbreviated form.

YHWH

The Jewish name for God, translated into the Roman alphabet.

The soul

In many religions there is the belief that people, and in some cases animals, have a kind of inner spark, which is separate from their body and mind, and which corresponds to the spirit described earlier. It is often called the spirit or soul. It is considered the most important part of a person's being because it is what can lead towards the Absolute and it is immortal (never dies).

High places are often significant in religion. It is as though they are trying to reach beyond the physical world towards the spiritual.

The people in this photograph are Buddhists, about to climb a sacred mountain in Sri Lanka.

The big questions

Religions ask and try to answer certain important questions: why was the world created? How should people live? Why is there so much suffering? What happens after death?

Jews, Christians and Muslims have a similar creation story: God created the world and made the first man, Adam, from soil, and the first woman, Eve. Adam and Eve lived in paradise but God cast them out to struggle on earth because they disobeyed Him by eating the fruit of a forbidden tree.

Adam and Eve as they are often shown in Christian paintings.

Any answers to the big questions posed by religions cannot be tested by reason and proved; the questioner has to trust or have faith in the answers. Another word for religion is faith.

Rules for behavior

The word religion comes from the Latin *religio*, which means an obligation or duty. Religions require their believers to behave according to a set of guidelines or rules.

Many religious people believe that the code of behavior was laid down by their God and must be obeyed without question.

Others believe the code should be adjusted to the times and circumstances in which they live.

For example, most religions teach that human life is sacred. Some religious leaders are against people using contraception to limit the size of their families. Many other religious people believe that contraception is a good thing, especially as the world is now so overcrowded.

Is it right to try to reduce population growth?

Freedom from suffering

Religions recognize that the world and the people in it are imperfect and a source of suffering. According to many religions, if people have faith and follow the religion's teachings correctly, then they will be saved from their wrongdoings and spared any further suffering after death by being united with the Absolute. This is often referred to as salvation or liberation. Some religions teach that liberation is possible even in this life.

This statue is of the Buddha, founder of Buddhism. Images of the Buddha sitting like this are seen as a symbol of spiritual growth which raises people above the suffering of the world.

Scriptures

Religious writings are called scriptures and are treated with great respect by believers. This is especially so when the scriptures are thought to have been communicated directly by God. Such direct communications are known as revelations.

The Muslim holy book, the Koran, is said to have been revealed by God.

Interpretation of scriptures

People who believe that every word of a certain scripture comes directly from God and so has unchanging authority for all time are known as conservatives, traditionalists or fundamentalists.

Other people may believe that the same scripture was inspired by God but feel that the social conditions of the time when it was written and the individual views and personality of the authors have to be taken into account in understanding it. These people are sometimes called liberals.

Christians disagree over the issue of women priests. Traditionalists argue that the scriptures imply that priests should be male. The liberals say there is no evidence for this.

Women were allowed to become priests in the Church of England in 1994.

Priests

Many religions have priests: officials who have public duties such as leading acts of worship. They may also try to guide people toward the spiritual world and in some religions act as a kind of go-between between people and God and vice versa.

Worship

Worship involves honoring God or the gods. Believers often meet together to express the feelings of wonder, joy and gratitude that they share. When the meeting takes the form of a ceremony it is often called a service. It is through the set actions performed in worship, which are known as rituals, that people demonstrate their beliefs.

Common rituals of worship are to cover the head as a sign of modesty and equality with other worshipers, and to kneel or bow down to show respect for God. In some religions, usually those that originated in hot, dusty countries, people also wash and take off their shoes.

A Muslim worshiping.

Prayer and meditation

In religions with a personal God, prayer often consists of giving praise and thanks, or asking for help and guidance for oneself or other people.

Prayer can also take the form of meditation. The aim of meditation is to achieve inner stillness so that barriers to understanding fall away.

Aids to concentration are often used in prayer and meditation. Common aids in many religions include beads, candles and incense.

A Hindu holy man in meditation.

Important life events

Religions usually celebrate important events in people's lives such as birth, reaching adulthood, marriage and death with special ceremonies. The aim of these is to encourage people to think about the meaning and purpose of life, and to help individuals through times of change. There is also the hope that those taking part will be looked upon favorably by the supreme power.

A Sikh wedding

Monks and nuns

In many religions there are groups of people who have different, stricter rules of behavior. The men (monks) live in monasteries and the women (nuns) in nunneries, separated from the rest of society. They do not marry or have ordinary jobs. Often they are not allowed to touch money. Some live lives of prayer or meditation; others do charity work.

Monks and nuns dress in the way they do as part of their aim to lead simple, modest lives, avoiding vanity and with everyone enjoying equal status.

A Christian nun

A monk of the Jain religion in India.

As part of the Jain belief in non-violence, the monk sweeps the ground to avoid stepping on living creatures and wears a mask to avoid breathing them in.

Festivals

Religious festivals often celebrate special events in the history of a religion, such as the birth or death of a leader. They also celebrate key events in nature, such as spring or harvest time. Festivals remind believers of their faith at certain times during each year and bring them together to give thanks for those things they consider valuable.

The Chinese New Year takes place near the end of winter and welcomes in the spring. Noisy processions and dancing are intended to frighten off evil spirits.

Sacred places

Some places, such as the mountain on page 4, are thought to have a spiritual quality, often because important religious events took place there, and believers try to visit them.

Jerusalem, in Israel, is sacred to Jews, Christians and Muslims alike, though for different historical reasons.

Jerusalem: the domed building is a mosque (Muslim place of worship); the wall on the bottom right is what remains of an ancient Jewish temple.

A journey to a sacred place is known as a pilgrimage. If the journey is difficult, it is often thought to strengthen a person's faith all the more.

The functions of religion

Religious people feel that what they believe in is true. People who study religions say that, true or not, they have many functions in society.

Some people say that religions were useful once, as a way of trying to make sense of human experience, but that they are no longer relevant, now that there are scientific explanations for things not previously understood. Others feel that science and religion can coexist.

Since the discovery of DNA in the mid-20th century, much more is known about how living things reproduce. This does not stop people from still feeling that the creation of new life is miraculous.

People who study how early humans lived in social groups see religion as a force which held communities together because it gave their members a shared code of behavior and a shared way of understanding the world.

Psychologists look at the way religion reduces people's fears by giving them something beyond themselves to rely on. Some think this is a healthy way of coping with a difficult world. Others think it prevents people developing confidence in their own abililties and stops them facing up to the harsh reality of the human condition.

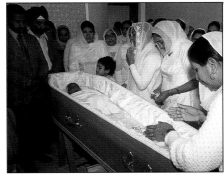

Religious funerals, like this Sikh one, can provide comfort and hope. Sikhs believe that everyone will eventually return to God.

Many people today are most interested in the way religions use stories, symbols and art to reach the deeper meanings beneath surface events.

These Hindu children are acting out a famous Hindu story about love. Religious stories can be relevant to people no matter what their beliefs.

The future of religion

Although in the richer, developed countries of the world, religion may be in decline, over the world as a whole, religions are actually growing. Some people claim that consumerism has become the new religion of the richer countries, with people's purpose in life being to earn enough money to buy more and more of the material possessions they worship.

Have the big stores become the modern equivalent of churches?

It has been predicted that there will eventually be a swing away from this materialistic outlook and back to the more spiritual values of religion.

Other points of view

People who do not believe in the existence of a supernatural power are called atheists.

Agnostics say that it is impossible to know whether God exists or not, because there is no proof either way. As this is the case, they do not think it is worth building their lives on vague beliefs.

Humanists believe that human beings have the capacity within themselves to develop and flourish, and to build a world which will be happier, more just and caring.

7

THE IMPACT OF RELIGION

Religion has been a powerful force in the development of different cultures around the world. In many places religion still has a major influence today.

In India, religion plays an important part in everyday life. Hindus often pause to worship at the roadside as they pass statues of the gods.

Even in Western societies where many people have no real religious commitment, religion still has some influence. For example, many public holidays are still held at the times of Christian festivals and some people argue against opening shops on Sunday because it is the Christian holy day.

Although Christmas is a Christian festival, many people today celebrate it in a non-religious way.

Some nonreligious people feel that religion has had a bad, rather than a good, influence on societies, causing wars for instance. Many religious people would argue that it is not religious ideas themselves which have had a bad effect, but the way in which these have been misinterpreted and misused, often by people in power, for personal gain. Sometimes problems which appear to be religious are really just as much to do with racism, and both religious and racial issues are bound up with politics.

Religion and the state

In the past, societies were often organized along religious lines. The word hierarchy literally means a ranking of people according to their spiritual authority. In Europe, kings and queens claimed to rule by "divine right": they were God's representatives on Earth. In Japan, emperors claimed to be related to the sun goddess, Amaterasu, and were worshiped right up until 1946.

The goddess Amaterasu

Some countries, such as Iran, are still governed by religious leaders today and many countries have an official, state religion which affects aspects of life there such as the law and education. Britain, for example, has Christianity as its state religion and state school assemblies have to include Christian worship. The USA does not have a state religion and religious education is not included in state schools.

School assembly in Britain.

Power

Religious leaders have sometimes abused their power, just like any other leaders may do, for personal gain. If leaders claim to be God's representatives, people may be too frightened to challenge them.

People have sometimes been scared into obedience by talk of what will happen to them after death. In Christianity for example, especially in the Middle Ages, leaders exploited people's belief that they may be condemned to burn forever in hellfire.

People dress up in devil masks at a Christian festival in Mexico.

In Christianity and Islam, the devil, or Satan, is seen as the personification of evil, who can tempt people away from God.

8

Reformers

While religious power has sometimes been abused, there have also been many movements and individuals inspired by their religion to try to change things for the better.

Gandhi

In the first half of the 20th century, Mahatma Gandhi struggled for the rights of black and poor people, and campaigned for India to become independent of British rule; in line with his strong Hindu beliefs, he insisted on achieving his aims without any violence.

A lot of charity work has been undertaken by religious people who feel they have a duty to help those who are in trouble. Many organized charities have religious origins, for example Salvation Army (Christian) and Muslim Aid. Religious charities are often given permission to work in areas that would be forbidden to others, for example in war zones.

The logo of Muslim Aid, which gives help to victims of poverty, war and natural disasters.

In Islam there is a very strong obligation for people to help the poor by giving a certain percentage of their money every year (see page 40).

War

Rulers have often encouraged their people to go to war by appealing to their religious beliefs. The rulers' motives may sometimes have included the desire for greater political power for themselves.

An example of this are the Crusades. Between the end of the 11th and 13th centuries, European Christian armies went on a series of armed pilgrimages. Their aim was to capture Palestine (now Israel), which was known to Christians as the Holy

Christians (on the left) and Muslims (on the right) fighting during the Crusades.

Land because Jesus was born there. Although these armed pilgrimages were called crusades or holy wars, they were really just as much wars of conquest against the Muslim Turks, who ruled Palestine at that time.

Some religions teach that no war can ever be justified and that believers should never take up arms for any cause. This belief is called pacifism. The Jain religion is pacifist; so are some Buddhist and Hindu groups; so, too, are some Christian-related groups such as Quakers and Jehovah's Witnesses (see pages 58 and 59).

Persecution

Where followers of a religion exist in smallish numbers and do not have much power, they sometimes suffer persecution. Other groups of people may ridicule their beliefs, without understanding them, and try to make them scapegoats for things which go wrong in society. This attitude is often accepted by the rulers because it deflects criticism away from their own failings. Religious prejudice is often combined with racism.

When the Jewish people lived scattered in different parts of Europe in the Middle Ages, they became targets for prejudice. Their persecution culminated in the Holocaust of World War II (see page 20).

A Russian Jewish family forced to leave their home in the 19th century.

Separatism

Some religious groups prefer to live as separately from others as possible in order to keep their traditions intact. This may be because of certain rules for living laid down in their scriptures, or it may come about because they feel threatened by persecution.

For example, the Amish are a group of Christian fundamentalists (see page 5) in North America. They live simple lives with strict rules, in communities separated from the rest of society. They will not take part in government and reject modern technology as evil.

Most religions have some areas of life in which they prefer to keep separate from others. For example, almost all religions prefer their followers to marry someone of the same religion.

The Amish refuse to have cars.

Women

The role of women is being debated in religions today. Historically, many religions have not given women a very high status and have excluded them from aspects of religious life. This is generally because women did not have a high status in the societies where the religions first developed. Although this may now have changed in society at large, conservative branches of religions often resist change because certain traditions are thought of as having been laid down by God.

In Saudi Arabia, a strongly Muslim country, women are not allowed to drive, even though this is not forbidden in Islamic scriptures because cars had not been invented at the time when they were written.

God as shown in a Christian painting. God is often still referred to as male, especially in Judaism, Christianity and Islam.

Education

Almost all religions emphasize the need for education and see it as their duty to promote learning. In the past, many people were taught to read and write by religious officials, so that they could study the religion's scriptures.

Muslim children studying the scriptures in Mauritania, West Africa.

The sun is at the center of the universe.

Sometimes, however, knowledge which might weaken religious belief is suppressed. In the 17th century, the Italian scientist, Galileo, supported the discovery that the earth moves around the sun and not vice versa. The Christian authorities in Italy made him publicly deny this claim or face torture: they were afraid that people would lose their faith if they knew that the earth was not the center of the universe, as they believed it said in the Bible.

Art

Many religious ideas are difficult and abstract, and people have always tried to express such ideas in works of art, together with the feelings they inspire.

Many works of art now in museums were originally produced to inspire religious faith, with the artists paid by religious officials. Before people were educated enough to be able to read, paintings and sculptures were a way of teaching a religion's key beliefs.

This Buddhist wall-hanging tells the life story of the Buddha.

Music and dancing

Most religions teach that the most effective kind of worship is that which involves a person's whole being, body as well as soul. This has led to religious music being composed and performed, and to special religious dances.

Music helps to create an atmosphere in which people can feel and express emotions such as awe and joy. Both music and dance can tell stories and can also be a way of entering into a trancelike state of meditation by repeating rhythmic sounds or movements.

Some religious groups disapprove of music and dancing because such physical pleasures are thought to be a distraction from the spiritual.

Tibetan monk playing a trumpet at a festival.

Hindu dances tell stories about the gods. The dancers make gestures, known as mudras, each of which expresses a particular idea.

Architecture

Nearly every religion has a special building where worship takes place. Great care is often taken to make this place beautiful so that it is felt to be worthy of the faith and will encourage praise and spiritual contemplation. Communities contribute money or labor to the building.

In the past, the wealth and feats of engineering which went into constructing places of worship were quite stunning, considering how much less technologically developed societies were then than they are now. Often, the place of worship became the focal point of a whole town or village.

The mosque called the Dome of the Rock in Jerusalem, which was built in 691.

The spread of religions

Some religions feel that they have a duty to try to convert others to their beliefs, either by preaching or by example.

Islam spread so far so fast (see page 42) after it was first founded at the start of the 7th century that the next six centuries became known as the Golden Age of Islam.

European Christian missionaries (people with a mission to convert others) started working extensively in South and Central America in the 16th century, and in Africa and Asia in the 18th century. They worked as teachers and in health care, but their main aim was to convert people from their existing beliefs to Christianity.

In recent years, some people in the Western world have become interested in Eastern religions such as Buddhism and Hinduism. These religions have been brought to the West especially by young people who have traveled in the East.

Many Westerners are attracted by the calming and uplifting effects of yoga, which is practiced by Hindus.

The Hare Krishna Movement is a Hindu group in the West. They believe that spiritual awakening comes from worshiping God, whom they call Krishna (see page 14), by meditating, chanting, singing and dancing. They take vows to be vegetarian and not to smoke, or drink alcohol, tea or coffee.

Followers of the movement are often seen in groups on Western streets.

Followers of the Hare Krishna Movement often worship in the street.

The men wear robes and often shave their head as a sign of devotion to the spiritual world, rather than the physical one. The women wear saris.

The movement is also known as the International Society for Krishna Consciousness (ISKCON).

Sects and cults

Strictly speaking, a sect is a group which breaks away from an established religion. A cult is a group which follows certain particular rituals of worship. All the major religions started off as sects or cults, but both words have come to be used in a derogatory sense because many people feel that certain modern sects and cults are unhealthy.

Some psychologists think that such groups appeal to people who are unhappy and feel themselves to be outsiders. These people, often young, see in a sect or cult the promise of a sense of purpose and of belonging to a group.

Unfortunately, they sometimes become so attached to the group that they will do anything the leader tells them to, even to the extent of breaking off all contact with their family.

The Unification Church is often seen as this type of cult. Members are nicknamed Moonies after their leader, Sun Myung Moon.

Marriage is extremely important in the Unification Church. Mass weddings are held, with marriage partners suggested by Moon.

HINDUISM

Hinduism is the world's oldest living religion, dating back to at least 2000BC. As its name suggests, Hinduism developed and still flourishes mainly in India. There are over 500 million Hindus in the world today.

How Hinduism began

The beginnings of Hinduism have been traced back to an ancient civilization known as the Indus Valley Civilization, which flourished between 3500 and 1500BC. This civilization came to an end at about the same time as a nomadic people, called Aryans, invaded India. Hinduism developed from the religious ideas of both these peoples.

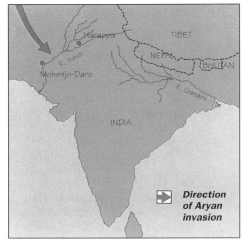

Direction of Aryan invasion

What is known about the Aryans comes mainly from a collection of hymns known as the Vedas.

What is known about the religion of the Indus Valley People comes mainly from finds made at the cities of Harappa and Mohenjo-Daro.

The god shown on this seal from Mohenjo-Daro is thought to be an early form of a Hindu god: Shiva (see page 15).

Hindu temples are often richly decorated with figures of gods and goddesses.

This is a sacred Hindu word: "Om" (see page 17) written in Tamil, a south Indian language.

This is just one of four gateways to a Hindu temple, not in India but in Kuala Lumpur, Malaysia.

This temple was built as recently as 1873, in a similar style to many temples in southern India.

This creature is a door guardian.

A varied religion

Hinduism is a very varied religion because of the way it developed over a long period of time and because it had no individual founder. The story told below gives some idea of its variety.

A mysterious beast appeared in the Land of the Blind. The king sent his courtiers to investigate. They waited until it was asleep and then warily touched it.

"It's like a wall," said the man feeling the elephant's side.

"It's like a spear," said the man touching the tusk.

"... like a fan" (the ear).

"... like a tree" (the leg).

"... like a snake" (the trunk).

"... like a rope" (the tail).

The blind men are, of course, all describing parts of the same thing. In the same way, the different types of Hinduism can sometimes seem so different as to be different things altogether.

For many Hindus, however, beneath all the variety there is one unchanging reality. This is called Brahman.

Brahman

Brahman is the absolute, unchanging, ultimate reality which many Hindus believe exists beyond the everyday world of appearances. Some Hindus see Brahman as God. Others see Brahman as an impersonal power which is beyond all description.

Legend has it that a wise man taught his son about Brahman by asking him first to put some salt into water and then to take it out again. Of course, the salt dissolved and the son could not take it out. His father then told him that the presence of Brahman in the world is like the salt in the water: invisible but everywhere.

Learning about Brahman by dissolving salt in water.

Atman

Hinduism teaches that each individual has a soul, called Atman. Many Hindus see Atman (self) as part of Brahman (the Absolute). For others, Atman is not part of Brahman; Atman and Brahman are identical: they are one and the same.

Birth, death and rebirth

According to Hinduism, living things do not have just one life but are all trapped in an endless cycle of life, death and rebirth. This cycle is called samsara. Another word for rebirth is reincarnation.

Samsara is seen as difficult and pointless, and Hindus hope eventually to be freed from it.

The symbol of a wheel, known as the wheel of life, stands for samsara.

Karma

The power which keeps the wheel of life spinning is called karma. Karma refers to the actions performed by each individual during a lifetime. A good action takes the person toward a better rebirth. A bad action takes them toward a poorer rebirth.

It is possible for a human being to be reborn as an animal. It will then be much harder for them to gain the knowledge they need to escape from samsara.

Release

Release from the cycle of rebirth and suffering (see above) is called moksha. Someone can achieve moksha only when they replace their ignorance with wisdom.

What prevents people from doing this is maya. Maya is the tendency to see things the wrong way, as in this story.

A man thought he saw a snake in his room. In his panic, he did not look at it closely but rushed around trying to escape and warning other people. If he had only examined the "snake", he would have found that it was just a harmless piece of rope.

What people fail to notice when they look at the world is the way it really is beneath the surface.

For many Hindus the only truly real things are Brahman and Atman. The rest is illusion.

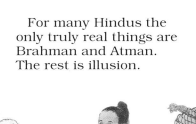

13

Many gods

Hindusm has many thousands of gods. Hindus believe the gods are all expressions of Brahman. For many Hindus however, worshiping the gods themselves is more important than the abstract idea of Brahman.

Goddesses play a key role, not only as wives of the gods but in their own right. They are often seen as creative power or energy.

Creation and re-creation

The main Hindu gods are Vishnu and Shiva. They are two of three gods thought to be responsible for the creation, preservation and destruction of the world. This cycle of change is thought to happen over and over again endlessly.

Brahma has four heads and sees in all directions.

Vishnu is the preserver and Shiva is the destroyer, also known as the liberator because he makes re-creation possible. The creator and least significant of the three gods is Brahma (not to be confused with Brahman).

Vishnu

Vishnu has ten incarnations, or avatars. These are the different forms in which he appears in the world, especially when danger threatens. The most important avatars are the seventh and eighth, Rama and Krishna, who are important gods in their own right.

The tenth and last avatar, Kalki, has not yet appeared. It is

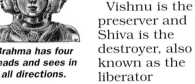

The third avatar of Vishnu: Varaha, the boar.

This painting shows Vishnu sleeping on a many-headed serpent in the ocean of eternity, between creations of the world. A lotus flower springs from his navel and Brahma emerges to create the world. With Vishnu is his wife, Lakshmi, goddess of wealth and beauty.

said that Vishnu will appear in this form at the end of the present age to destroy the wicked and re-establish order.

Hindus sometimes look upon leaders of other faiths as avatars of Vishnu. They may call Buddha, Jesus or Muhammad avatars.

Rama

Rama and his wife, Sita, represent the ideals of male and female behavior.

Rama

One popular story tells how Sita was kidnapped by the demon king, Ravana, and taken to his fortress in Sri Lanka. Helped by the monkey god, Hanuman, Rama rescues her.

An effigy of Ravana.

Krishna

Krishna is perhaps the most popular of all the gods. Many stories about him emphasize his mischievous nature when young, especially when he was acting as a cowherd.

Krishna's favorite cowgirl was called Radha. The story of their love for each other is a model of how followers should devote themselves to their god.

This painting shows Krishna with some cows. Krishna is often shown playing a flute.

Cows are considered sacred in Hinduism and are not killed for beef. One reason for this may be that cows are great providers, for example of milk, butter and dung (used for fuel).

Shiva

Shiva, the destroyer or liberator, is often shown in statues as Lord of the Dance (Nataraja). Shiva combines both male and female qualities.

Shiva's four arms indicate both his power and the idea that a god cannot be put into ordinary human form.

His upper right hand holds a drum on which he beats out the rhythm of his dance: the dance of liberation and re-creation.

His upper left hand holds a naked flame. This represents his power and also the discipline with which he manages it.

Shiva has a third eye in the middle of his forehead. This represents wisdom. It looks inwardly, not outwardly.

Shiva dances inside a hoop of flames. This represents the energy of the universe and its creatures.

Shiva is dancing on the defeated figure of a demon. The demon represents ignorance.

Ganesha

Ganesha is an important minor god of Hinduism. The son of Shiva and his wife, Parvati, he is often worshiped at the start of any new undertaking, such as going on a journey, because he is thought to remove obstacles.

Ganesha was beheaded by his father. According to one story, this was to punish his mother for showing off his beauty as a baby. Later, Shiva gave him an elephant's head instead.

His big ears can listen to everybody's prayers.

His potbelly represents wealth and success.

Parvati, Durga, Kali

Three goddesses are associated with Shiva. Parvati is a beautiful and gentle wife, complementing the compassionate side of Shiva's nature.

Parvati

Durga and especially Kali are fierce and powerful: a match for Shiva's more destructive side. Durga, the Inaccessible, slays demons with a sword. Kali is known as a destroyer of evil.

Kali

15

Duty

Hindus try to live according to their dharma, which is the code of behavior or duty which governs a person's life. An individual's duty is determined by their position in society and by the stage of life they have reached.

Place in society

Four main social groupings, known as varnas, are described in Hindu scriptures. These are, first: priests and teachers, who are called brahmins; second: rulers and the military; third: merchants; and fourth: manual workers. Each group has its own code of behavior.

In the past, there has been some confusion between the religious idea of varnas and the political idea of the caste system. According to the caste system, people were divided up into thousands of different groups and people of certain groups were discriminated against. This is illegal in present-day India.

A brahmin priest

Four stages of life

The stages of life described in the scriptures are the student, the family man, the recluse and, finally, the wandering holy man who cuts free of all family ties, owns nothing and simply lives

A Hindu holy man.

by begging. The goal of this final stage is singlemindedly to seek union with Brahman.

The four stages are a model of how people ought to live but they are very much an ideal.

Yoga

There are four main types of yoga in Hinduism. Individuals can choose whichever type best suits their stage of life and temperament.

Karma yoga is the discipline of action. It involves a person working hard to fulfill their dharma.

Bhakti yoga is the discipline of devotion. It means offering wholehearted love and prayer to a personal god.

Jnana yoga is the discipline of knowledge, and involves study.

Raja yoga is the discipline of the mind. It involves practicing techniques of mental self-control, including meditation.

All types of yoga can include physical exercises for self-discipline.

Temples

Although there are many temples in India, Hindus only attend at set times on holy days and at festivals. Otherwise, they go to temple rituals as they please.

For Hindus who live in western countries, temples have become more important as places to meet and worship together.

Hindu temple in London.

Worship

Worship takes place mainly in the home and tends to bring the whole family together. It is focused on a shrine, like the one in the picture below.

Which god or gods are important to someone will depend partly on family background and the region where they grew up, as well as individual preference.

For some Hindus, the images of the gods are used to help focus the mind beyond the individuality of the gods and onto Brahman.

The shrine contains objects which match the five senses of sight, hearing, smell, taste and touch. The aim of this is to involve the whole person in the worship.

A picture or statuette of a god or goddess is kept on a small table. The statue here is of the god Krishna, with his flute. The painting shows the goddess, Lakshmi.

Offerings of incense, food and flowers have been placed in front of the images. The food will later be shared between the worshipers.

A bell is rung to help the worshipers to focus their minds.

Incense

Ganges River

The Ganges, along with many other rivers in India, is considered sacred. People often have their ashes scattered in the river after cremation. It is an important place of pilgrimage.

Pilgrims bathing in the Ganges to purify themselves.

Focusing on a yantra, or mandala, like the one below, the meditator's concentration is drawn toward the invisible point at the center of the interlocking triangles. This point represents Brahman.

Festivals

Divali is associated with the goddess, Lakshmi, and is held at the Hindu New Year, which falls in November. Divali means the festival of lights. Light represents knowledge. Numerous lamps and candles are lit everywhere and people exchange presents and cards.

People paint geometric designs, called rangoli patterns, outside their homes for Divali.

The yearly festival of Dassehra commemorates Rama's victory over Ravana (see page 14). Key moments from the life of Rama and Sita are retold in dances and plays.

Prayer beads

This is the sacred word "Om". A sound-symbol, or mantra, for Brahman, it is recited over and over again. There may also be singing.

The spring festival of Holi celebrates the tricks Krishna, as cowherd, used to play on the cowgirls. There are processions, bonfires and dancing, and people scatter and squirt colored powder and water over each other.

Sacred writings

All the sacred books mentioned below were written in Sanskrit, the language of ancient India. Nobody knows exactly when they were compiled, as it was so long ago. All were written before the start of the Common Era, some over a period of several centuries.

The Vedas were passed on by word of mouth for centuries before being written down. The oldest and most sacred of the four Vedas is the Rig Veda, containing over a thousand hymns.

"Thou art that" in Sanskrit, a phrase repeated in the Upanishads. It identifies Atman with Brahman.

The Upanishads consist of philosophical teachings about Brahman and the struggle to achieve moksha.

The adventures of Rama and Sita are described in the Ramayana, which means the life story of Rama.

The Mahabharata is probably the longest poem in the world, with over 100,000 verses. It tells of the struggle between two related, ruling families. The best known and most popular part of this epic tale is the Bhagavad Gita.

In the Bhagavad Gita, Krishna appears on the battlefield as charioteer to the hero, Arjuna. He advises Arjuna about the different ways of seeking moksha, and identifies the different types of yoga.

Arjuna

Krishna

JUDAISM

Judaism is the faith of the Jewish people, who live all over the world but share a history. Unlike people of other religions, Jews are born into their faith. Anyone born of a Jewish mother is counted a Jew, whether or not they observe Jewish religious practices.

Nearly half of the world's 14 million Jews live in the USA, a quarter in Israel and a quarter in Europe.

One God

The history of the Jews goes back about 4000 years, when they were a nomadic people called the Hebrews, living in what is now the Middle East.

One Hebrew, Abraham, is seen as the father of the Jewish faith because he championed its central belief: the belief in one God. Neighboring peoples worshiped several gods.

Chosen people

Jews believe that God chose them to be his special people and made a covenant (contract) with Abraham.

Abraham and his wife, Sarah, were sad because they had no children. One night, Abraham heard God telling him not to worry: he would have as many descendants as there are stars in the sky and they would live in a land of their own: the Promised Land. Soon after this, a son, Isaac, was born.

Isaac's son was called Jacob or Israel and the descendants of Abraham became known as Israelites.

(The Jewish practice of circumcision dates from the time of Abraham and is done as a sign that a boy is descended from him.)

Abraham hears God's voice.

According to the covenant, God promised to care for the Israelites, but in return they must obey Him.

The Exodus

In about 1250BC the Israelites escaped from Egypt, where they were being used as slave labor. This escape, known as the Exodus, is of great importance in the history of Judaism. This is how it is said to have happened.

God chose a man called Moses to plead with the Egyptian pharaoh (king) to free the Israelites. When Pharaoh refused to listen, God sent a series of plagues to make him relent. The tenth and last plague was the most terrible. One night all the eldest sons of the Egyptians died, while the Israelite boys were saved. Pharaoh gave in.

The plagues included frogs, flies and locusts.

The Israelites set off on their journey but Pharaoh sent his army in hot pursuit. When they reached the Red Sea, the water miraculously parted, making a way for the Israelites. As soon as Pharaoh's army began to cross, the water closed up and all his horses and men were drowned.

God's laws

After their escape from Egypt, the Israelites spent some time wandering in the desert. During this time, God renewed the covenant with them and gave them a set of laws to live by. There are hundreds of Jewish laws but they all stem from these first ten commands, known as the Ten Commandments.

God is said to have given the laws to Moses, carved on tablets of stone, at a place called Mount Sinai. This painting from the Middle Ages shows Moses bringing the Ten Commandments to the Israelites.

The Ten Commandments

Worship no god but me.
Do not make for yourselves images (to worship).
Do not use my name for evil purposes.
Observe the Sabbath (holy day).
Respect your father and mother.
Do not kill.
Do not commit adultery.
Do not steal.
Do not accuse anyone falsely.
Do not be envious of other people's possessions.

The picture below shows the Western Wall in Jerusalem.

People stand in front of the wall to pray.

Jewish boys celebrating a festival at the Western Wall.

This man belongs to a Jewish sect called the Hasidim. This originated in 18th century Poland. Its male followers still wear 18th century Polish dress.

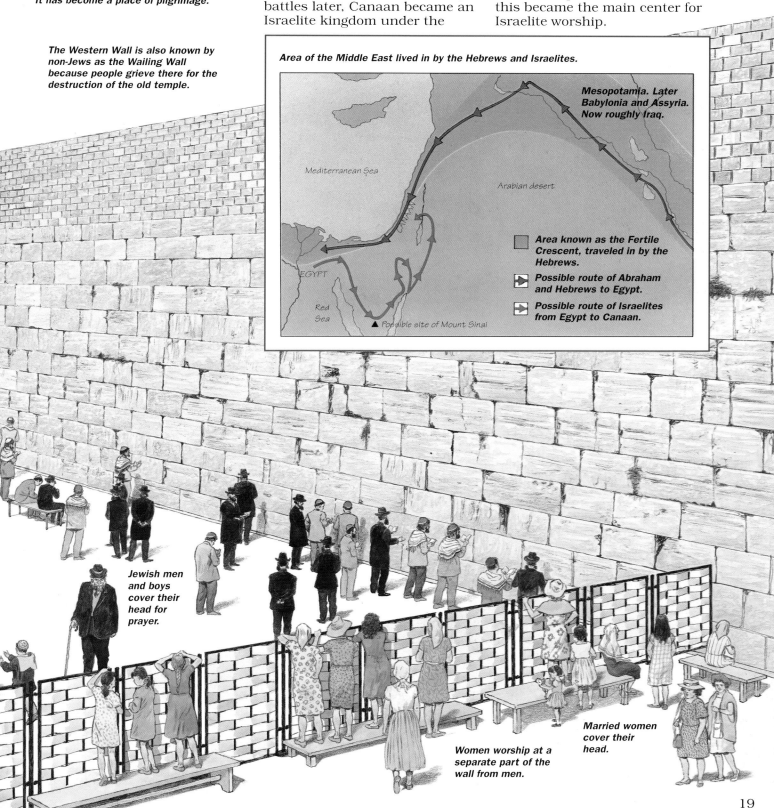

The Promised Land

About forty years after the Exodus, the Israelites reached Canaan, which they believed was the Promised Land.

Two hundred years and many battles later, Canaan became an Israelite kingdom under the Israelite king, David. He established a capital city at Jerusalem in 993BC.

David's son, King Solomon, built a temple at Jerusalem and this became the main center for Israelite worship.

The Western Wall is the only remaining part of an ancient temple which was destroyed by the Romans (see page 20). It has become a place of pilgrimage.

The Western Wall is also known by non-Jews as the Wailing Wall because people grieve there for the destruction of the old temple.

Area of the Middle East lived in by the Hebrews and Israelites.

Mesopotamia. Later Babylonia and Assyria. Now roughly Iraq.

Mediterranean Sea

Arabian desert

CANAAN

EGYPT

Red Sea

▲ *Possible site of Mount Sinai*

Area known as the Fertile Crescent, traveled in by the Hebrews.

Possible route of Abraham and Hebrews to Egypt.

Possible route of Israelites from Egypt to Canaan.

Jewish men and boys cover their head for prayer.

Women worship at a separate part of the wall from men.

Married women cover their head.

The prophets

Once the Israelites became settled in Canaan, they did not always keep faithfully to the Law. The prophets were people who reminded the Israelites of their covenant responsibilities and warned them of the consequences of disobedience.

They were often champions of the poor and needy, arguing that being God's chosen people gave the Israelites increased responsibility for others.

The prophet Isaiah, as shown in an Italian mosaic.

Exile in Babylon

From the mid 8th century BC onwards, Canaan, now known as Israel, was ruled by many different peoples, including the Assyrians, the Babylonians and the Romans.

In 587BC, the temple in Jerusalem was destroyed by the Babylonians, and many Israelites were taken into exile in Babylon. Jerusalem was in an area called Judah and the exiled Israelites now became known as Jews.

The Jews began to follow the laws given to Moses even more strictly, in order to preserve their identity. For instance, they were very strict about keeping the Sabbath day and following certain food laws. Outsiders were suspicious of the Jews because of these different traditions, which they did not recognize or understand.

The Diaspora

By the 1st century BC, Israel was under Roman rule. In 70AD, in response to a Jewish rebellion, the Romans destroyed a second temple which had been built in Jerusalem; they outlawed Jewish education and killed any Jews who tried to teach. For the second time, many Jews were driven out of Israel.

The Romans carrying off treasure from the Jerusalem temple. The seven-branched object is a candlestick called the menorah. Known as the everlasting light because it was kept lit at all times, the menorah became a symbol of Judaism.

The exiles joined existing Jewish communities around the Mediterranean, spreading to Spain and Portugal, and eventually into eastern and central Europe. This dispersion or "scattering" of the Jews became known as the Diaspora. Today the word is used to refer to all Jews outside Israel.

The Middle Ages

In the centuries following the Diaspora, the Jews suffered further persecution, especially at the hand of Christian rulers.

The Christian world was prejudiced against Jews for both religious and economic reasons. Jews do not recognize Jesus as the son of God like Christians do. The Jews were also accused of making money out of other people's debt. This came about because Christians were forbidden by their religion to lend money and charge interest on it, so this became a service provided by Jews, who were barred from many other professions.

After years of ill treatment, Jews were expelled during the late Middle Ages from England, from France and even from Spain, where they had previously flourished. In countries where they were allowed, Jews were often forced to live in separate and inferior areas called ghettos.

Prejudice against Jews, which is called anti-Semitism, continued well beyond the Middle Ages and right into the 20th century. Between 1871 and 1907, Jews in Russia were the victims of large-scale massacres known as pogroms. Many fled to the USA or Palestine. (Palestine was the old land of Israel, renamed by the Romans.)

In the Middle Ages many Jews in Europe were forced to wear special clothes to single them out from Christians.

The Holocaust

The worst-ever persecution of Jews took place as recently as World War II (1939-1945) and is known as the Holocaust. Then, six million European Jews (more than one third of the total world population of Jews) were brutally murdered by the Nazis, who were in power in Germany under the leadership of Adolf Hitler.

This sculpture in Jerusalem is in memory of those who died in the Holocaust.

The modern state of Israel

During the 19th century, Jews had begun to resettle in Palestine. A group of Jews called Zionists began to campaign for a separate Jewish state to be set up within Palestine.

After the Holocaust, this seemed important for Jewish survival. In 1948 Palestine was divided up, and the modern state of Israel was founded. Jews from all over the world have made their home there.

The creation of Israel inevitably led to hostility between Israelis and non-Jewish Palestinians (mainly Muslim Arabs) and between Israel and surrounding countries, which were also mainly Muslim. Efforts to find a lasting solution to the Israeli-Arab conflict still continue today.

Israel and its neighbors.

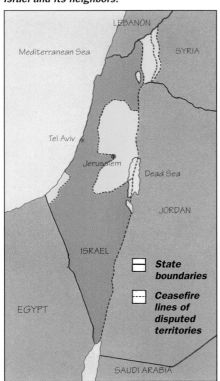

State boundaries

Ceasefire lines of disputed territories

The Messianic Age

Out of the Jews' early history arose the hope of a leader sent by God and called the Messiah, who would re-establish a Jewish kingdom and an age of peace. Some Jews believe that the establishment of the state of Israel marked the beginning of the Messianic Age.

Sacred writings

The Tenakh is a collection of books, known to Christians as the Old Testament (part of the Bible). Although some of the material they contain was being passed on by word of mouth from around the time of Moses, the books are thought to have been written down over about 900 years, from 1000 to 100BC. They were written mainly in Hebrew.

The first five books of the Tenakh are called the Torah, which means teachings. They contain the teachings which God gave to Moses.* Tradition has it that the Torah was written by Moses, but scholars have shown that the material came from various sources.

The Tenakh also contains histories, prophecies, poems, hymns and sayings.

Copies of the Torah for use in synagogues (see page 22) are not in book form but in scrolls. Even today, they are not printed but are each copied out by hand.

The Talmud is a vast collection of writings compiled in the first few centuries AD. It consists of the thoughts and discussions, some of them humorous, of about 2000 rabbis. A rabbi is an expert on the Torah.

Orthodox and Progressive Jews

Religious Jews are either Orthodox or non-Orthodox.

Orthodox Jews accept the Torah (see above) and all its laws as being God's word to Moses, to be obeyed without question. Non-Orthodox Jews accept that human beings played a part in devising the laws and they have attempted to adapt Judaism to modern life. Non-Orthodox Jews are also known as Progressive Jews and, depending on what country they are in, Conservative, Reform, Liberal or Reconstructionist.

Extremely Orthodox Jews are known as ultra-Orthodox. The Hasidim (see page 18) are an example of an ultra-Orthodox sect.

The difference between the types of Jews is largely seen in styles of worship and in the clothes worn by men.

Small boxes like this are called tefillin and contain prayers. For worship, Orthodox Jews strap one round their head, another round the arm nearest their heart. This is to remind them to worship God with both head and heart.

Skull cap

Tefillin strap

Jews cover their head when praying. Many Orthodox men wear a skull cap (kippah) all the time, as a sign of being always in the presence of God.

Prayer shawl

Many Jews put on a prayer shawl to worship. Orthodox Jews often wear a fringed garment all day under their ordinary clothes. The fringe is to remind them to obey God's law.

*Nowadays, the whole of Jewish teaching is sometimes referred to as the Torah.

Synagogues

The word synagogue means a meeting place. Synagogues are Jewish centers of worship, education and socializing.

Torah scrolls are kept in a cupboard or alcove called the ark. This is named after a wooden chest which is said to have held the covenant given to Moses on Mount Sinai.

A light hangs in front of the ark. It represents the old menorah (see page 20) and God's everlasting presence.

Torah scrolls are often covered with a mantle when not in use.

To save the Torah from getting soiled during readings, the text is not touched A pointing stick is used instead.

The second of the Ten Commandments forbids images of God, so there are no pictures or stained glass windows showing God.

A six-pointed star, called the star of David, is an important Jewish symbol and may be seen inside or outside synagogues. Despite its name, the star has no direct link with King David.

Worship in the synagogue consists mainly of prayers and readings, especially from the Torah. The worship is often led by a rabbi or a singing leader called a cantor.

In Orthodox synagogues, women sit separated from men; the service is in ancient Hebrew, the readings are chanted and no musical instruments are used.

In Progressive synagogues, men and women sit together; part of the service is in the local language and singing may be accompanied by an organ. Women can become non-Orthodox rabbis.

Language

Although Jews have always learned to read ancient Hebrew, so that they can read the Torah and prayers in the synagogue, Hebrew had died out as a living language until early in the 20th century. Then, a Jewish settler in Palestine, called Ben Yehuda, set about reviving it. By refusing to speak anything but Hebrew to his family and fellow settlers, he began the development of modern Hebrew. This differs slightly from ancient Hebrew and is now Israel's official language.

A carving of the Ten Commandments in ancient Hebrew.

Another language, called Yiddish, is a mixture of ancient Hebrew and medieval German. It is still spoken today by some ultra-Orthodox groups.

The home

The Jewish home is even more important than the synagogue for ensuring the continuation of the Jewish faith.

Many families have a mezuzah similar to this one on their door. A mezuzah contains a text from the Torah.

In Orthodox homes especially, food must be prepared in accordance with God's laws to make it "kosher" (fit). Meat and milk products must never be eaten at the same time or prepared with the same utensils, and many foods, including pork

Bar and bat mitzvah

At the age of 13, a boy is considered an adult for religious purposes and is called bar mitzvah (son of the covenant). This is marked by a ceremony in the synagogue, followed by a party. Many synagogues hold a bat mitzvah (daughter of the covenant) ceremony for girls when they reach the age of 12.

A boy at his bar mitzvah with his father and the rabbi.

Festivals

The Torah forbids pork and shellfish.

and shellfish, are forbidden by the Torah.

Meat must be drained of blood because the blood is seen as the life of the animal and so is too sacred to be eaten. Animals are slaughtered by a special method which is designed both to drain the blood and kill with the minimum amount of pain.

The Sabbath

The Sabbath (Shabbat in Hebrew) is the Jewish holy day, which begins at sunset on Friday and lasts until nightfall on Saturday. It is a day for rest and contemplation. No work is done because the Jewish creation story says that God made the world in six days, then rested on the seventh.

The Sabbath meal is prepared in advance of Friday evening. The meal is a family occasion with special songs, readings and a prayer of thanksgiving.

People go to the synagogue during the Sabbath and the day ends with a ceremony at home.

Rosh Hashanah is a festival for the Jewish New Year, which falls in September or October.

The main ceremony at Rosh Hashanah is the sounding of the shofar, a ram's horn, blown to "wake" people so that they can prepare to lead better lives.

Ten days after the Jewish New Year comes Yom Kippur or the Day of Atonement (making amends). This is the most sacred day in the Jewish year, spent in prayer, fasting and asking God's forgiveness for wrongdoings.

Passover, or Pesach, held in March or April, marks the night when the Israelite children were saved or "passed over" by the plague, before their escape from slavery in Egypt (see page 18).

The most important ceremony is the seder, a meal in which some of the food and drink has a special meaning.

The story of the Exodus is read from a book called the Hagadah, in response to a ritual question from the youngest child: "Why is this night different from other nights?"

An egg symbolizes new life or a new beginning.

A roasted lamb bone is a reminder of the eve of the Exodus: God told the Israelites to daub lambs' blood on their doorposts as a signal to the angel of death to pass over them.

The bitter taste of horseradish is a reminder of the misery of slavery.

Salt water symbolizes tears.

Unleavened bread (made without yeast) is eaten. Bread made with yeast takes time to rise and on the eve of the Exodus the Israelites only had time to make the unleavened type.

At Hanukkah, the festival of lights, held in November or December, a candlestick with nine branches is used.

*The woman of the house lights candles to welcome in the Sabbath and she says a blessing.
A special candle is also lit to mark the end of the Sabbath.*

Wine is drunk as a symbol of joy and the Sabbath meal always includes two plaited loaves.

The smallest candle is used to light one candle a night over eight nights, until all of them are burning.

BUDDHISM

Buddhism was developed in India by a man called Siddattha Gotama, who lived about 2500 years ago. He became known as the Buddha, which means the enlightened one, because of his wisdom. It is estimated that there are now over 500 million Buddhists in the world, mainly in countries to the east of India.

A time of change

At the time of Siddattha Gotama's birth, many Hindus were looking for new answers to certain questions, especially the question of suffering. Why must people suffer? How can it be avoided? This was a particularly serious problem for Hindus because of their belief in rebirth, which meant suffering not just in one life but in many (see page 13). Siddattha became interested in the problem and set about finding new ways of solving it.

Born a prince

Siddattha was probably born in about 563BC. His father was the ruler of a small kingdom in northern India, near what is now Nepal. His family were Hindus.

Siddattha in his chariot.

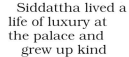

The four sights

According to one legend, a fortune teller predicted that the young prince would be a great emperor provided he was prevented from seeing four sights: a sick man, an old man, a dead man and a monk. If, however, he were to see these things, he would take up the life of a wandering holy man. Siddattha's father vowed to keep all such sights well away from his son.

Siddattha lived a life of luxury at the palace and grew up kind and generous. He married and had a son. Then, just when his life seemed complete, he began to question the value of living in idleness and luxury. One day he went for a drive in his chariot outside the royal park and he saw the four sights.

The search

Siddattha realized that even the most rich and powerful ruler cannot escape the suffering caused by illness, old age and death. He saw the fourth sight (the monk) as a sign that he should leave the palace and search for an answer to the problem of suffering. He became a wandering holy man.

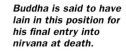

Siddattha as a holy man.

This statue of the reclining Buddha is in a temple in Rangoon, Burma.

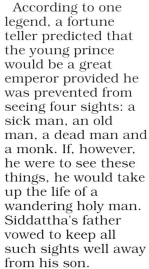

Buddha is said to have lain in this position for his final entry into nirvana at death.

The search led Siddattha from one extreme to another. He studied with some holy men, but this did not lead him to an answer. He then followed a strict fast for six years. This left him exhausted and near death. He then realized that the problem of suffering would not be solved by going to extremes and he vowed to adopt what he called the Middle Way: neither indulging in luxury, nor causing undue hardship to his body.

Siddattha fasting

Enlightenment

Siddattha sat in the shade of a fig tree at a place called Bodh Gaya and remained there for many days, deep in meditation. Then, as dawn broke one day, he saw the meaning of all things unfold: he was enlightened. From this point on, Siddattha is known as the Buddha.

Nirvana

At the moment of his enlightenment, Buddha attained nirvana. This is freedom from the cycle of rebirth, and so freedom from suffering. Buddhists say that nirvana cannot be described in words; it lies beyond the definable.

Buddha went on to live to the age of 80. When he died, he became known as the Tathagata, one meaning of which is Thus-gone. This describes the state of nirvana after death, where the person cannot be reborn and neither exists nor does not exist.

The first teaching
Buddha passed on his new-found knowledge to a group of monks at Sarnath, near Benares. His main teachings consist of what are known as the Three Universal Truths, the Four Noble Truths and the Eightfold Path (see next page).

This 18th century painting shows Buddha teaching for the first time.

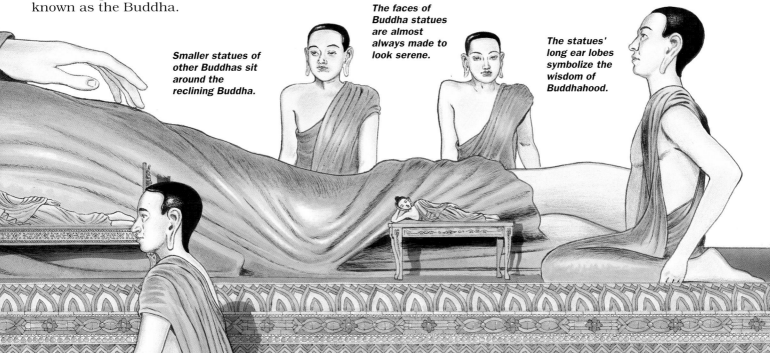

Smaller statues of other Buddhas sit around the reclining Buddha.

The faces of Buddha statues are almost always made to look serene.

The statues' long ear lobes symbolize the wisdom of Buddhahood.

The Three Universal Truths

1. Everything in life is impermanent and constantly changing. Buddha's thinking about this is similar to that of the Greek philosopher, Heraclitus, who said that it is impossible to step into the same river twice.

2. Because nothing is permanent, life is unsatisfactory. People desire and become attached to things which cannot last. Even if someone achieves a state of contentment, it will not last. Indeed, knowing that the contentment must end is itself a source of suffering.

To Buddhists, suffering means not only the great pain and tragedies which people experience. It also means all those things which make life less than perfect.

3. There is no eternal soul, and what people call the self is simply a collection of changing characteristics. Buddha compared the self to a chariot, which is simply a collection of parts assembled in a certain way. It can easily be taken apart.

The Four Noble Truths

1. All life involves suffering.
2. The cause of suffering is desire and attachment.
3. Desire and attachment can be overcome.
4. The way to overcome them is to follow the Eightfold Path.

The Eightfold Path

This is the moderate Middle Way followed by Buddha in his own search for enlightenment. It is a code for living.

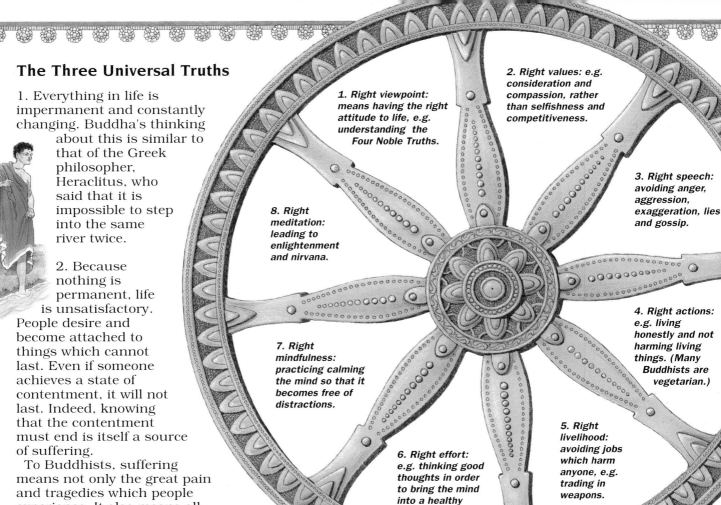

1. Right viewpoint: means having the right attitude to life, e.g. understanding the Four Noble Truths.

2. Right values: e.g. consideration and compassion, rather than selfishness and competitiveness.

3. Right speech: avoiding anger, aggression, exaggeration, lies and gossip.

4. Right actions: e.g. living honestly and not harming living things. (Many Buddhists are vegetarian.)

5. Right livelihood: avoiding jobs which harm anyone, e.g. trading in weapons.

6. Right effort: e.g. thinking good thoughts in order to bring the mind into a healthy state.

7. Right mindfulness: practicing calming the mind so that it becomes free of distractions.

8. Right meditation: leading to enlightenment and nirvana.

An eight-spoked wheel is used in Buddhism to represent the steps of the Eightfold Path.

Meditation

Most Buddhists consider meditation essential in achieving nirvana. It is through searching within the self during meditation that the individual can come to understand the truth of Buddha's teaching. Often meditation involves concentrating on the idea of impermanence and change.

Many Buddhists believe that almost anything can be a focus for meditation and they talk of doing everyday things in a "mindful" way. By this they mean that people should concentrate on the present moment and so not be distracted by lots of conflicting thoughts.

Buddhist monasteries often have a meditation room which people can visit.

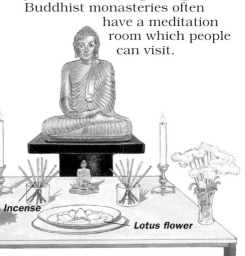

In a meditation room, offerings of flowers and incense are placed in front of a statue of Buddha. The statue and offerings serve as a focus for the meditators.

Incense

Lotus flower

The lotus flower

A common symbol in Buddhism is the lotus flower, which has its roots in mud at the bottom of ponds. Buddhists say that people should aim to be like the lotus. The mud represents human life; the pure flower symbolizes enlightenment.

Lotus flower

The question of God

For Buddha the need for an answer to the problem of suffering was too urgent to waste time in empty speculation. He did not try to answer the questions of whether God exists, or why and how the world was created. To do this, he said, would be like a man wounded by an arrow refusing to relieve his pain until someone told him how many feathers the arrow had or the color of the hair of the man who fired it.

The three jewels

Most Buddhists are united in their belief in the Buddha, in his teachings, which are called the dhamma, and in the holy order of the sangha (see above). These are known as the three jewels because they are so precious. They are sources of help and support to people, and so are also known as the three refuges.

Sacred writings

It was not until some time after Buddha's death that his teachings were written down. At first they were passed on by word of mouth.

One important collection of writings is called the Tipitaka (the Three Baskets). This consists of the Buddha's sayings, comments on the sayings, and rules for monks. It was written during the 1st century BC in Sri Lanka.

The Tipitaka was first written on palm leaves which were collected together in baskets.

The sangha

Sangha is the name given to any community of Buddhist monks or nuns. The group of monks who heard Buddha's first sermon at Sarnath were converted and formed the first sangha. Buddha is said to have been unsure at first whether to have women in the sangha but he was persuaded to by his mother-in-law, who begged to be allowed to join.

It is the custom even today in certain Buddhist countries for boys to spend some time living as monks. This may be for as little as a few days or as long as a few years.

This boy is dressed for the ceremony which will admit him to a monastery.

The fine clothes are a reminder of Buddha's life as a prince.

Now the boy wears monk's robes and his head has been shaved.

He carries a begging bowl, one of his very few possessions while in the sangha.

The spread of Buddhism

Buddhism spread from its birthplace of Bodh Gaya to many other eastern countries, where it is still practiced today. In India itself, it more or less died out fairly quickly. Some experts think it was reabsorbed into Hinduism, once reforms were made to that religion as a result of Buddhist criticism.

Soon after Buddha's death, differences of opinion began to arise among his followers. These eventually developed into separate kinds of Buddhism. The two main types of Buddhism practiced today are Theravada and Mahayana (see next page).

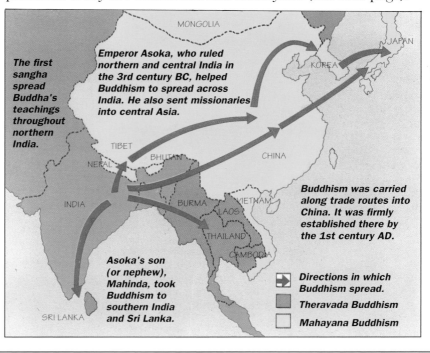

The first sangha spread Buddha's teachings throughout northern India.

Emperor Asoka, who ruled northern and central India in the 3rd century BC, helped Buddhism to spread across India. He also sent missionaries into central Asia.

Buddhism was carried along trade routes into China. It was firmly established there by the 1st century AD.

Asoka's son (or nephew), Mahinda, took Buddhism to southern India and Sri Lanka.

Directions in which Buddhism spread.
Theravada Buddhism
Mahayana Buddhism

Theravada Buddhism

Theravada means teachings of the elders. Theravada Buddhists believe that they follow Buddha's original teachings more closely.than other groups do.

They look upon Buddha as a remarkable person and a perfect model to imitate but believe

A Theravada monk

he was only human. When he died, he ceased to be able to offer practical help to people still alive. For this reason, Theravada Buddhists do not pray to the Buddha. They believe that individuals must make their own way by following the teachings in the Tipitaka.

The sangha is very important to Theravada Buddhists and they believe that people who are not monks will be less successful in their search for enlightenment.

Mahayana Buddhism

Mahayana Buddhists believe that the Buddha can respond to appeals from people today. They see him as one of many Buddhas of the past, present and future. Also, they believe in bodhisattvas: people who are on the brink of enlightenment but who have chosen to stay in the world for the sake of helping others towards the same state.

Mahayana Buddhists use other texts as well as the Tipitaka.

While the sangha is important, becoming a monk is not essential, as it is possible to move toward nirvana while still involved in society.

The bodhisattva of compassion.

As Buddhism spread throughout Asia, Mahayana Buddhists adapted to the different cultures they met. This led to the development of distinctive branches of this type of Buddhism. Three of these are Vajrayana, Pure Land and Zen.

Vajrayana Buddhism

To help them towards nirvana, Vajrayana Buddhists chant mantras and use mandalas (see page 17) in meditation.

Mantras are often carved on prayer wheels like the one this boy monk is turning. Each time the wheel spins, the mantra is considered "said".

Vajrayana Buddhism is also known as Tibetan Buddhism because it used to flourish in Tibet. Its leaders there had political power as well as religious influence. Then, in the 1950s, Tibet was overthrown by China, a Communist country which did not allow religion. Many Buddhists had to flee. The leader of Vajrayana Buddhism, who is called the Dalai Lama, still lives in exile in India.

The Dalai Lama used to have his headquarters in part of this palace at Lhasa in Tibet.

Pure Land Buddhism

Pure Land Buddhism began in China and spread to Japan in about the 13th century. The central figure is a bodhisattva known as Amida Buddha. He was so full of compassion that he took a vow that anyone calling on his name when they died would be reborn in the Pure Land. This is a place in which it would be easy for everyone to follow Buddha's teachings and reach nirvana.

Amida Buddha

Zen Buddhism

Like Pure Land, Zen Buddhism began in China and spread to Japan in about the 13th century. The name Zen means meditation and Zen Buddhists try to spend as much time as possible meditating.

A monk meditating in a Zen garden. The patterns on the gravel ground are to help concentration.

Zen Buddhists also use riddles, called koans, such as this: what is the sound of one hand clapping? The purpose of koans is to contradict people's usual patterns of logical thinking so that they see beyond preconceived ideas and so attain enlightenment.

Sacred writings are less important in Zen than in other types of Buddhism.

Buildings

Temples exist in all Buddhist countries but it is not considered essential to go to them to worship.

Some sacred Buddhist buildings are called pagodas. These are often in the form of a tiered tower, especially in Japan and China.

Pagodas and structures called stupas are often found next to temples.

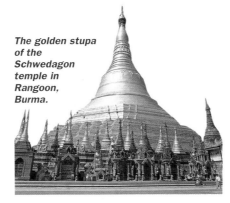

The golden stupa of the Schwedagon temple in Rangoon, Burma.

A pagoda in Nikko, Japan. The spire symbolizes wisdom, rising above the physical world.

A stupa is a sealed mound containing what are said to be remains of Buddha or copies of his teachings. Stupas are often bell-shaped. Visitors pay their respects to Buddha by walking around the mound.

Places of pilgrimage

Some of the main places of Buddhist pilgrimage are those associated with important events in the Buddha's life: his birthplace (Lumbini Grove), the place of his enlightenment (Bodh Gaya), the place of his first teaching (Sarnath), and the place of his death (Kusinara).

Festivals

Wesak is the celebration of Buddha's birth and, in Theravada countries, of his enlightenment and death, too. Statues of Buddha are decorated and, in China, bathed in scented water. Offerings are taken to monasteries and there may be a firework display.

Vassa (meditation retreat) takes place during the rainy season. In Buddha's day, traveling was impossible at this time, so he told the monks to stay in one place to study and meditate. Ordinary people also try to put aside time for study and meditation during Vassa. At the end of the retreat, people take offerings of new robes to monks.

Celebrations also take place to mark Buddha's first teaching. In Sri Lanka the festival of the Sacred Tooth is held. One of Buddha's teeth is paraded through the streets.

Festival of the Sacred Tooth at Kandy in Sri Lanka. Buddha's tooth is carried in a miniature stupa on the back of an elephant.

CHRISTIANITY

Christianity is the religion of Christians. They believe in the teachings of a man called Jesus, who was given the title Christ by his followers. Christ is Greek for the Hebrew word messiah (see page 21). One of its meanings is savior. For Christians, Jesus is the son of God: God in human form. They believe he came to earth to save everyone from their wrongdoings (called sins in Christianity). He did this by sharing in human suffering and sacrificing his life.

Christianity began in what is now Israel. Today it is found in most parts of the world, especially in Europe, North and South America, Australia and New Zealand. With well over 1000 million followers, it is the world's largest religion.

Jesus' birth

Jesus was born a Jew in Roman-occupied Palestine about 2000 years ago. The story of his birth emphasizes his humble earthly background.

According to Christian scriptures, God sent an angel, Gabriel, to announce to a young woman called Mary that she would be Jesus' mother. Many Christians believe that Mary was a virgin, despite being a mother.

Jesus was born in Bethlehem, where Mary and her fiancé, Joseph, had gone to pay their taxes. The town was crowded and they had to stay in a stable. It was here that the baby was born.

The first people to visit the baby Jesus were shepherds. In another version of the story, wise men follow a star to the stable and bring three gifts: gold for a king, frankincense (a good-quality incense) for a holy man and myrrh (a bitter incense) for someone who will suffer and die.

Mary and Joseph on their way to Bethlehem.

The stained glass window below is in Augsburg Cathedral, Germany.

The picture on the bottom left shows the Annunciation: the angel Gabriel's announcement to Mary that she will be Jesus' mother. Above Gabriel is God, sending Jesus down to Mary.

The top picture shows Mary being crowned Queen of Heaven. Behind her are God and Jesus. The bird is a dove, symbolizing the Holy Spirit (see page 33).

The picture on the bottom right shows the Nativity (Jesus' birth) with Mary, Joseph and Jesus in the stable.

Jesus' baptism

Jesus grew up in Nazareth and probably became a carpenter. Then, at about the age of 30, he asked his cousin, John, to baptize him in the River Jordan. Baptism involved being immersed in water as a sign of washing away sin and the start of a new life.

John recognized Jesus as the savior people had been waiting for.

Jesus is baptized.

Jesus' work and teaching

Jesus chose 12 disciples (followers) and started teaching. He gained a reputation for healing sick people and for performing miracles, for example feeding a crowd of five thousand on only five loaves and two fish.

The Jewish religious authorities felt threatened by Jesus' popularity and by some of the things he and his disciples did; for example, they made a point of helping the outcasts of society, non-Jews (known as Gentiles) and women. Jesus also forgave sins, which they believed only God could do.

The loaves and fish. The fish became a symbol of Christianity.

Jesus taught that people should repent of their sins and make a fresh start. This was necessary before God's kingdom could be established here on earth. In God's kingdom, there would be justice and peace, and people would be freed from suffering. Jesus taught that love and serving others were more important than the Jewish law and he spoke of God as "Father". Speaking of God in such a familiar way had never been heard of before.

Jesus washed his disciples' feet to show his willingness to serve others.

The parables

Jesus often taught by telling parables. These are stories which teach a spiritual lesson. One parable, called the Prodigal Son, shows that God is a loving father who readily forgives his children their sins. Here is the story.

A man had two sons. The younger son demanded his share of his inheritance, left the country and squandered the money, having a wild time. When famine hit the land, the only way he could survive was to work on a pig farm and eat the pigs' food.

Realizing that his father's laborers had more food than they could eat, he decided to go back home, admit his faults and ask if he could become one of the laborers.

His father was so

The prodigal son returns home.

overjoyed to see his long-lost son that he threw a party. This annoyed the dutiful elder brother. The father explained to the elder brother that everything he possessed had always been his to share, but the younger brother had been lost and was now found, and this must be a cause for rejoicing.

In Jerusalem

Three years after he began teaching, Jesus took the disciples to Jerusalem for the Passover festival (see page 23) even though he knew that the growing hostility of the Jewish religious leaders would lead to his death.

In Jerusalem, many people welcomed him as a king; they hoped that he would overthrow the Romans and re-establish a Jewish kingdom. When they realized that this was not to be, they turned against him.

The Last Supper

Jesus shared a last meal with his disciples, during which he tried to warn them of what was about to happen. He asked them to keep his memory alive by continuing to share bread and wine together after his death. The bread was to symbolize his body and the wine his blood, which would be sacrificed for their sake. (See "Transubstantiation" in the Glossary on page 62.)

The Last Supper, as shown in a 15th century Italian painting.

The crucifixion

Judas, one of Jesus' own disciples, handed Jesus over to the Jewish religious leaders. Jesus was charged with blasphemy, which means treating God's name with disrespect. The Roman governor, Pontius Pilate, who alone had the power to sentence people to death, was worried about a Jewish uprising and so gave in to their pressure. He ordered Jesus to be crucified: to be fastened to a cross until he died. Two thieves were crucified alongside him.

The crucifixion of Jesus, as shown in a painting. The two figures at either side of Jesus may be his mother, Mary, and one of the disciples.

This 14th century painting in Norwich Cathedral, England, shows the resurrection of Jesus and his ascension. The artist has given the people in the painting 14th century clothes.

The resurrection

Jesus was buried in a tomb, but on the third day after his crucifixion, the tomb was found empty. Some followers said that they had seen Jesus and the news spread that he was resurrected (risen from the dead).

The ascension

Jesus is said to have appeared to his disciples several times before going up into heaven to be reunited with God, his Father. His ascent into heaven is known as the ascension.

Many Christians today believe that when they die, they will achieve salvation and their soul will go to heaven to be with God and Jesus. Heaven, or paradise, is seen as a state of bliss.

The Bible

Christian teaching is written in the Bible, which is in two parts: the Old and New Testaments. Another word for testament is promise or covenant.

The Old Testament is almost the same as the Jewish Tenakh (see page 21) and tells of the covenant which Jews believe God made with them through Abraham and, later, Moses (see page 18).

The New Testament was written in Greek and tells of a new covenant which Christians believe God made with all people through his son, Jesus Christ.

The New Testament is made up of four gospels (gospel means good news), numerous epistles (letters) and two other books.

In the Middle Ages, monks used to make beautiful handwritten copies of the Bible. This is the beginning of one of the books in a 12th century Bible.

The new covenant

The Old Testament teaches that salvation comes through keeping God's law. The New Testament teaches that salvation comes through believing in the death and resurrection of Jesus Christ.

The central message of the new covenant is that although Jesus was without sin, he paid the price for human sin with his own life. His resurrection is seen as a sign of God's forgiveness and salvation of all humanity.

The epistles

These are the earliest Christian documents, written about 30 years after Jesus' death. Most of them were written by a formerly very strict Jew called Saul. He changed his name to Paul after a dramatic conversion in which he was temporarily blinded by a vision of the risen Christ. Paul traveled

A mosaic showing Paul.

throughout the Roman Empire, telling non-Jews about Jesus and setting up Christian communities known as Churches. His letters give advice and encouragement to these early Christians.

The gospels

The gospels were written between 70 and 150 years after Jesus' death by the four evangelists called Matthew, Mark, Luke and John. Evangelist means announcer of good news. Each of the gospels gives an account of Jesus' life, teaching, death and resurrection from the point of view of its author. They were written with the intention of converting people to Christianity.

Mark writing his gospel.

Persecution

The Roman authorities persecuted both Christians and Jews, making them scapegoats for their own political disasters. The Roman emperor, Nero, ordered the destruction of Jerusalem in 70AD, with the intention of ridding the Empire of Christians and Jews alike.

Christians were sometimes persecuted by being fed to lions at public spectacles.

Constantine

In 313AD the Roman emperor, Constantine, converted to Christianity. He founded the city of Constantinople on the site of the old Greek city of Byzantium and made Christianity a legal religion.

In 325AD he summoned a council at Nicaea to draw up a definite statement of Christian belief. From then on, this was to be the accepted form of Christianity, known as Orthodoxy. This statement of belief was called the Nicene creed and included the doctrine of the Trinity.

This states that God is three persons: Father (the creator of all), Son (Jesus) and Holy Spirit (God's continual presence in the world). This is still a central Christian doctrine.

This painting shows the Trinity of Father, Son and Holy Spirit (the dove). Doves are often seen in Christian works of art. The figures around the edge are angels.

The split between East and West

In the 5th and 6th centuries, the Roman Empire split in two. Constantinople became the center of the Eastern or Byzantine Empire, while Rome was the center of the Western Empire.

In 1054 there was a dispute between the head of the Church in Constantinople (the Patriarch) and the head of the Church in Rome (the Pope). This led to a major split, called the Great Schism, between the two branches of the Church.

The Western Church later became known as Roman Catholic. (Catholic means universal.) The Eastern Church became known as Orthodox. Over the years, slight differences in belief and worship grew up between the two Churches and still exist today.

The division between Eastern and Western Christianity in 1054.

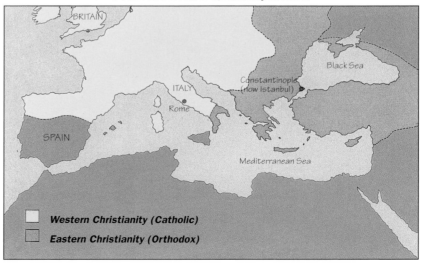

Western Christianity (Catholic)

Eastern Christianity (Orthodox)

The Reformation

The next major division in Christianity took place in the 16th century. A new "reformed" type of Church known as Protestant grew out of the protests of people like Martin Luther and John Calvin. They criticized some of the practices of the Catholic Church which they believed had become too rich and powerful, and corrupt.

Martin Luther

In 1517, the German, Martin Luther, attacked the authority of the Pope and Church leaders. He protested in particular about the sale of indulgences. This was the Church's custom of taking money from people and in return promising them that they would not be punished for their sins after death.

Martin Luther

Luther translated the Bible into German. Until then it had been read in Latin, which ordinary people did not understand. It was soon translated into other languages too. Luther believed that the teachings of the Bible and an individual's personal faith in Christ were more important than Church rituals.

John Calvin

A Frenchman, John Calvin, gave Protestantism its definite form, with his organized Church structure. Calvin shared Luther's ideas but also believed in predestination: the idea that God has a plan for each person, including whether or not they will be saved.

John Calvin

The Counter-Reformation

The Counter-Reformation was a reforming movement within the Catholic Church. It developed in response to the Protestant Reformation.

Many Europeans now returned to the Catholic faith but by and large Europe became divided into a Protestant north and Catholic south. There was hostility between Catholics and Protestants, with Protestants suffering persecution in Catholic countries, while in Protestant countries Catholics met with a similar fate.

Many people were burned at the stake for their beliefs in the 16th and 17th centuries.

The Church of England

In 1529, King Henry VIII of England challenged the supreme authority of the Pope and declared himself head of the Church in England. Under Henry's son, Edward VI, England became a Protestant country and many Catholics lost their lives. Henry's daughter, Mary I, returned the country to Catholicism, and in her reign many Protestants were killed.

Queen Elizabeth I, who reigned from 1558 to 1603, established a Church of England that was a compromise between Protestant and Catholic.

Today, branches of the Church of England, also known as the Anglican or Episcopalian Church, are found in many countries of the world. Those that follow a more Catholic tradition are known as "high Church" and those that follow a more Protestant tradition are known as "low Church".

Elizabeth I of England

Nonconformism

Some Protestants refused to conform to the established Churches of northern Europe, and in the 17th century, began to set up Nonconformist Churches. They believed that all links with Catholicism should be cut, that worship should be kept simple and churches plain, for example without statues.

The first Nonconformists in England were called Puritans.

One of the main Puritan groups were the Quakers. (See pages 58 and 59 for Quakers and other Nonconformist groups.)

The Pilgrims

Many Nonconformists, under threat of persecution, fled from Europe. The most famous group became known as the Pilgrims. They were among the very first European settlers in America. They sailed from Plymouth, England, in 1620 in a ship called the Mayflower.

During their first winter in America, about half of them died of starvation. With the help of the native Americans, the rest survived. After their first harvest they held a feast to thank God. Thanksgiving Day is still celebrated in America every November.

The Pilgrims arrive in America.

Methodism

One of the main groups of Christians to have grown out of the early Nonconformist movement are the Methodists, who are now found all around the world.

Methodism's founders were two English brothers, John and Charles Wesley. They preached the scriptures to large open-air congregations in the 18th century and won over many factory and farm workers.

Methodism got its name from the methodical habits of its members, whose goal was to lead ordered, disciplined lives. They campaigned for social reforms.

John Wesley preaching.

Churches

Christians are expected to go to church, although worship can take place elsewhere, too. The worship involves praising God or asking for God's help in prayers, hymns or chants. The Bible is read and there may be a sermon (talk on Christianity). The main act of church worship is held on a Sunday.

Many Catholic, Anglican and Orthodox churches are quite elaborately decorated, while Protestant churches tend to be plainer. A cathedral is the principal church of a region.

The picture below shows a typical Anglican church.

This is St. Basil's Cathedral in Moscow. Many Orthodox churches have onion-shaped domes like this.

Churches were traditionally built in the shape of a cross, like this one, as a reminder of Christ's crucifixion.

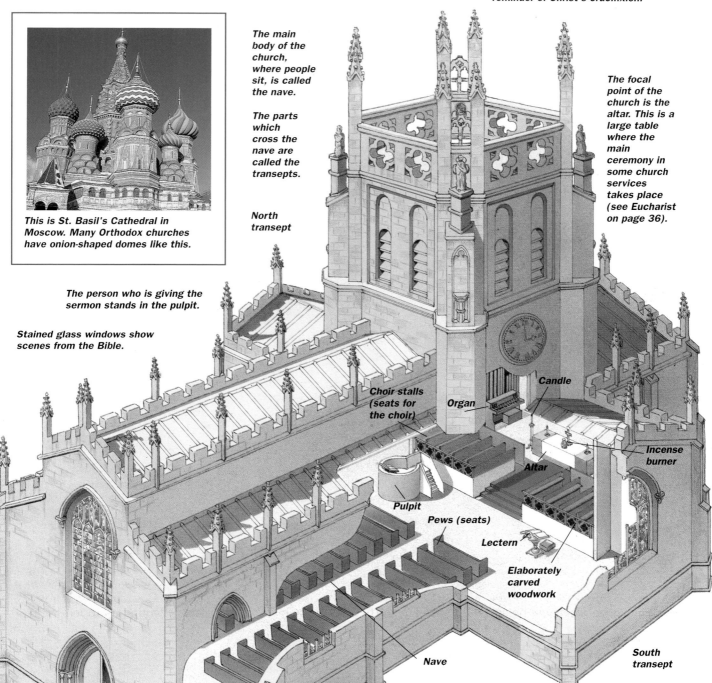

The main body of the church, where people sit, is called the nave.

The parts which cross the nave are called the transepts.

North transept

The focal point of the church is the altar. This is a large table where the main ceremony in some church services takes place (see Eucharist on page 36).

The person who is giving the sermon stands in the pulpit.

Stained glass windows show scenes from the Bible.

Choir stalls (seats for the choir)

Candle

Organ

Incense burner

Altar

Pulpit

Pews (seats)

Lectern

Elaborately carved woodwork

Nave

South transept

The Bible is read from a stand called a lectern.

The main entrance is at the west end.

This is a font, which has water in it for baptisms.

Many churches were built with the altar at the eastern end, known as the chancel, because this faced Jerusalem.

Priests and bishops

In Catholic, Anglican and Orthodox churches, services are usually led by a priest. The long, flowing garments priests wear are adapted from the style of dress worn in the Roman Empire, where Christianity first began. The "dog collar" may have been copied from the collars worn by slaves, signifying that the priest is a servant of God.

The overall head of a cathedral and its region is a bishop. A bishop carries a crosier, which is like a shepherd's crook. It is a reminder of his duty to look after his flock: the people in his region. A bishop's hat is called a miter.

Dog collar

Crosier

Miter

Priest   Bishop

The Eucharist

The Eucharist, which means thanksgiving, is the main service in many churches. It is a re-enactment of the Last Supper (see page 31) in which worshipers eat a small piece of bread or a wafer and sip a drop of wine.

This service has a slightly different significance for different branches of the Church and they call it by different names. It is usually called mass in Catholic churches, holy communion in some Anglican churches and the divine liturgy in Orthodox churches. Protestants often call it the breaking of bread or the Lord's supper.

Wine and wafers

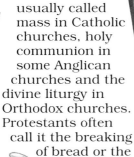

Baptism

People are welcomed into the Christian faith by a baptism ceremony (see page 31).

A baptism in a Greek Orthodox church.

Priest

In some branches of Christianity, baptism involves people having a little water poured on their head instead of being totally immersed. Some branches of Christianity baptize adult believers but most baptize babies. The baby's parents and godparents, who have been chosen by the parents, promise that they will bring the baby up as a Christian.

At an infant baptism, the baby is also officially given its Christian (first) names, which is why a baptism is sometimes referred to as a christening.

Confirmation

At a confirmation ceremony, a person becomes a full adult member of their church.

They take on the promises made on their behalf at baptism, and the local bishop lays his hands on their head to "confirm" the help of the Holy Spirit in living a Christian life.

The age at which people are confirmed varies.

A confirmation ceremony

Mary, mother of Jesus

All Christians honor Mary as Jesus' mother, chosen by God, but Catholic and Orthodox Christians give her a special role. They believe that if they pray to Mary she will intercede between them and Jesus. This means that she will plead with Jesus on their behalf.

A 19th century Ethiopian painting of Mary and Jesus.

Festivals

Christmas, the joyful celebration of Christ's birth, is held in the West on December 25th, although the date of Christ's birth is not known. The date was chosen by Emperor Constantine to coincide with a Roman sun festival. Many people think this is appropriate as Jesus is sometimes called the Light of the World. In the Orthodox Church, which uses a different religious calendar, Christmas is on January 7th.

In church at Christmas children often carry candles in oranges. These represent the Light of the World.

In church at Christmas, which means Christ's mass, the story of Jesus' birth is read, carols (Christmas hymns) are sung and there may be a model of the stable scene on display.

The customs of sending cards and decorating trees for Christmas began in the 19th century and have little real connection with Christianity.

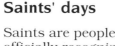

Easter, which falls in March or April and marks the death and resurrection of Jesus, is the most important Christian festival. The day of Jesus' death is called Good Friday because Christians believe that submitting to his crucifixion was an act of supreme goodness for humankind. They believe that the resurrection took place on the Sunday of that week.

Special church services are held at Easter, and in Catholic and Orthodox countries processions take place in the week leading up to Easter Sunday. This is known as Holy Week.

Saints' days

Saints are people who are officially recognized by the Catholic and Orthodox Churches as having lived particularly holy lives. Many saints are celebrated on the date of their death.

In some countries, for people who have the same Christian name as a saint, their saint's day is as important as their birthday, with cards, presents and a party.

Saint Francis of Assisi, in Italy, was a specially devout monk who died on October 4th, 1226. He is often remembered for his love of animals.

Easter coincides with and is named after an earlier, pre-Christian Spring festival. Easter eggs symbolize new life.

This photograph shows a Good Friday procession in Ecuador.

A statue of Christ carrying a cross is paraded through the streets. It is thought that Christ was made to carry his cross to the top of the hill where he was crucified.

The women are wearing the national costume of Ecuador.

Lent is the period before Easter when Christians remember their sins. It used to be a time of fasting but today people are more likely to try to give up something like cigarettes, alcohol, or chocolate. Lent commemorates a time when Jesus spent 40 days and nights fasting and praying in the wilderness.

In Great Britain, the day before Lent starts is Shrove Tuesday, also known as Pancake Day. Making pancakes was a way of using up food before the fasting period began.

On the first day of Lent, which is called Ash Wednesday, some Christians mark their foreheads with ash as a sign of repentance from sin.

Child with cross drawn on forehead in ash.

Whitsun, or Pentecost, comes seven Sundays after Easter and commemorates the official birth of Christianity. It marks the day when God's Holy Spirit is said to have descended on Jesus' disciples in the form of wind and fire. This event gave them the confidence to go out and convert people to Christianity.

The disciples at Pentecost. The Holy Spirit is shown at the top of the picture. The object held by the man at the bottom may be a prayer shawl (see page 21).

ISLAM

Islam means obedience, or peace through submission to the will of Allah (God). Followers of Islam are called Muslims, which means obedient ones.

There are about 1000 million Muslims in the world, mainly in the Middle East, North Africa and parts of Asia. Islam is the second largest religion after Christianity and is the fastest-growing religion in the world.

Muslims share some beliefs about God and about history with Jews and Christians. The most important event in Muslim history, however, was the revelation of God's word to a man called Muhammad in the early 7th century AD. Muhammad became known as the Messenger of God, or the Prophet.

Muslims at prayer

— *Shoes*

Muhammad's early life

Muhammad was born in Mecca, in what is now Saudi Arabia, in about 570AD. As a child he was orphaned and was brought up by a generous uncle. He grew up to be a camel driver, trader, husband and father; he was well respected in the community and was known as the Trusted One.

However, Muhammad's life was not completely happy. He disapproved of the lawlessness of his fellow countrypeople and was troubled because they worshiped many gods. Abraham's belief in one God (see page 18) had previously spread to Arabia but had been lost again.

Arabia in Muhammad's time.

God speaks to Muhammad

Muhammad used to retreat into the mountains to pray and contemplate. Around the time of his fortieth birthday, while he was in a cave on Mount Hira, near Mecca, he received his first revelation: God spoke to him through the angel Jibril (Gabriel). Muhammad continued to receive revelations throughout his life.

The migration

Muhammad began to preach his central message in Mecca, that "there is no god but Allah". People soon became interested in what he had to say and, afraid of his popularity and power, the political leaders began a hostile campaign against him. Eventually, in 622, Muhammad had to move his community of followers to a city now known as Medina, the City of the Prophet.

A story tells how Allah was with Muhammad during the journey. He and his friend, Abu Bakr, were hiding in a cave when they heard soldiers approaching. Abu Bakr was afraid but Muhammad reassured him that they would be saved. Just as one of the soldiers was about to enter and search the cave, he stopped, saying that there was no point. Right across the entrance was a massive spider's web. How could Muhammad and his friend have entered the cave without breaking the web?

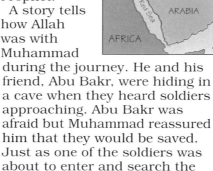

The journey to Medina is known as the Hijrah, or migration, and is such an important event that Muslims date their calendar from it. According to the Islamic calendar, it is now the 15th century. In Medina,

Muhammad's following grew very strong. In 629 the Muslims were able to conquer Mecca and Muhammad was finally accepted there as the Prophet of God. He won respect both as a great religious leader and as a statesman.

The death of Muhammad

After the death of Muhammad in 632, Abu Bakr made an announcement to those who could not believe that he had really died. He said: "Those of you who worship Muhammad must accept that Muhammad is dead. As for those of you who worship Allah, Allah is living and will never die." This shows the Muslim attitude to Muhammad. He is not to be worshiped. However, as Allah's messenger, he deserves the greatest respect. For this reason, whenever Muslims say Muhammad's name, they also say "Peace be upon him".

This photograph shows part of a mosque (see page 41), built in the early 17th century, at Isfahan in Persia (now Iran). Muslim countries were skilled in tile making and many mosques are decorated with mosaics.

Islamic art

The Koran forbids images of any kind to be made of Allah, Muhammad or the other prophets, or indeed of any person or animal. This is partly because the worship of images is forbidden in Islam, and partly because no artistic representation could possibly be good enough to reflect adequately the magnificence of Allah's creation.

For these reasons, Islamic artists have concentrated on developing beautiful geometric patterns and on calligraphy, because writing is so important, especially in the Koran.

The beliefs of Islam (see next page) can be written in calligraphy to form the shape of this boat, which is known to Muslims as the Ship of Life.

A Koran which was copied by hand in India in the 18th century.

Sacred writings

The Koran, also known as the Qur'an, is the holy book of the Muslims. It is believed to be the word of Allah revealed to Muhammad during the last 22 years of his life, so Allah, not Muhammad, is its author. At first the revelations were passed on by word of mouth, but it was not long before they were written down, although they were not collected into one volume until after Muhammad's death.

The Koran speaks of Allah's oneness and power, and about what Muslims should believe. It also gives detailed guidance on how they should live.

As the Koran is seen as the word of Allah, most Muslims try to learn to read it in its original Arabic, even if this is not their own language. Only about one sixth of the Muslims in the world are Arab.

Muslims learn several surahs, or chapters, of the Koran by heart and some try to memorize the whole book. They read some part of it every day and usually wash as a sign of respect before touching it. A set of writings called the Sunnah are reports of the words and deeds of Muhammad. They help to interpret the Koran and give additional guidance on belief, worship and behavior.

Reading the Koran. The book is often placed on a stand.

39

Muslim beliefs

Many Muslims divide their beliefs into six categories:

1 Belief in Allah.

2 Belief in angels.

3 Belief in the holy books. Muslims believe that other prophets (see below) besides Muhammad were given written revelations by God but that these no longer exist in their original form. They call Jews and Christians "People of the Book" out of respect for their belief in the Tenakh and Bible.

4 Belief in the prophets of the Tenakh and Bible, such as Adam, Ibrahim (Abraham), Musa (Moses) and Dawud (David). Muslims respect Isa (Jesus) as an important prophet, though not the son of God. Muhammad was the last of the prophets.

5 Belief in the Day of Judgment and life after death. On the Day of Judgment, the deeds of every human being will be weighed. Those whose good deeds weigh heavy will be able to cross a narrow pathway across hellfire and safely reach paradise.

6 Belief in predestination. This is the belief that God controls everything that happens. It is linked to the idea of obedience. Muslims try to do the will of Allah rather than following an individual path through life.

The Muslim code of behavior is based on the belief that all life is created by Allah and should therefore be respected. The code involves many social responsibilities such as respecting parents, neighbors and the community, and being honest, patient and trustworthy. It is forbidden in Islam to kill animals for sport.

The Five Pillars

The Five Pillars of Islam show how Muslim beliefs should be put into action in daily life.

1 The Shahadah. This is the declaration of faith, which is repeated several times a day: "There is no God but Allah, and Muhammad is His messenger."

The Shahadah written on a vase.

2 Salah. These are the five daily prayers which are said, in Arabic, at dawn, just after noon, mid-afternoon, just after sunset and after dark. The prayers may be said in any clean place and extra prayers may be offered at any time. They consist mainly of verses from the Koran, praising Allah and asking for His guidance.
Muslims wash and often take off their shoes before praying, for cleanliness.

Women must cover their head for prayer. Men do not have to, although many do.

Muslims always face the holy city of Mecca when praying.

They perform a set of ritual movements, including standing, bowing and kneeling, to show their submission to the will of Allah.

Prayer beads may be used to help concentration.

Unless they are in a mosque, Muslims pray on a prayer mat for cleanliness. Some modern prayer mats have a built-in compass for finding the direction of Mecca.

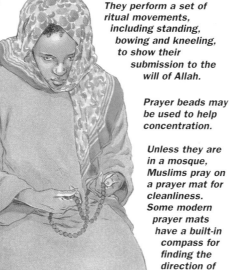

A box for collecting zakah money.

3 Zakah. This is the Muslim obligation, for those who can afford it, to give at least 2½ percent of their savings and other valuables every year to the poor.

4 Sawm. This means fasting. During the ninth Muslim month, Ramadan, Muslims eat and drink nothing during the hours of daylight. This reminds them that the good things in life are to be enjoyed but not over-indulged in. It also shows equality with the poor. Ramadan is a time for studying the Koran and for practicing self-discipline and charity.

5 Hajj. This means pilgrimage. Muslims hope to make a pilgrimage to Mecca once in their life, to visit the Ka'bah. This is a place of worship believed to have been built by Ibrahim and one of his sons, Isma'il (Ishmael). It had fallen into misuse but Muhammad restored it to the worship of Allah.
The Hajj takes place during the twelfth Muslim month, when millions of pilgrims travel to Mecca. They visit other important sites nearby too.
Nobody is allowed to go on Hajj without first making sure that their family is provided for in their absence. The poor, old, sick and disabled do not have to go.

The Ka'bah in Mecca.

Men have to wear white sheets to enter Mecca at Hajj. This is to show equality. Women sometimes wear them too.

Mosques

Mosques are for communal prayer and serve as centers for the community. Besides the main prayer room, there are rooms for washing, for studying and for teaching children. There are often fountains outside.

At the set times for the five daily prayers, verses from the Sunnah are relayed, often by loudspeaker, from one of the towers of the mosque. This acts as a call to prayer. The person who recites the verses is called the muezzin (mu'adhin).

All male Muslims are expected to attend the mosque on Fridays for noon prayers. Women who go to the mosque usually sit separately from men. The direction of Mecca is indicated by an arched alcove or a decorated panel in the wall.

The prayer leader is called the imam, which means man of knowledge. Imams are appointed by the mosque.

Star and crescent

Some mosques have crescents or crescents and stars on them. These have no real religious significance but came to be associated with Islam: the crescent because of Islam's lunar calendar; stars because the Koran speaks of stars as being among Allah's signs.

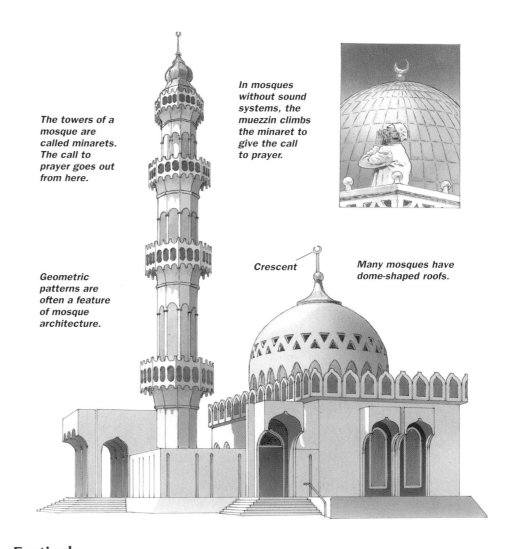

The towers of a mosque are called minarets. The call to prayer goes out from here.

In mosques without sound systems, the muezzin climbs the minaret to give the call to prayer.

Geometric patterns are often a feature of mosque architecture.

Crescent

Many mosques have dome-shaped roofs.

Festivals

Id-ul-Fitr is a festival which takes place at the end of the fast of Ramadan. People attend special prayers at the mosque and give food to the poor. They eat celebratory meals, visit friends and relations, and exchange presents and cards. This is a time of thankfulness for Allah's many blessings and for his help during the fast.

Id-ul-Adha is celebrated by Muslims who are at home while others are on Hajj. It commemorates an event reported in the Koran and also, in slightly different versions, in the Torah and in the Old Testament.

Ibrahim was asked by God to sacrifice his beloved son, Isma'il, to show his obedience. Just as Ibrahim was about to kill Isma'il, God provided a ram to take Isma'il's place. The festival celebrates both Ibrahim's faith and God's mercy.

At Id-ul-Adha an animal is slaughtered and the meat shared with the poor.

The Jihad

A person's inner struggle to live a good life is known as the Jihad. For many Muslims, the Jihad also includes the holy duty to try to win others over to Islam by setting a good example in their lives. They believe that the solution to world problems would be a worldwide Islamic state.

Muslim dress

Both men and women should dress modestly and not try to appear attractive to the opposite sex by displaying their bodies. Women should cover their head, arms and legs. In some places it has become the custom for women to cover their faces, too, when outside the home, although no hard and fast rules about this are laid down in Islamic scriptures.

Anything which threatens family life, such as the possibility of affairs outside marriage, is to be avoided, and men and women are not usually allowed to mix freely.

Dress rules are interpreted differently in different places and by different people.

Women wear veils in some countries.

Muslim diet

In Islam, all meat must be halal (permitted), which means it has to have been prepared in a certain way. The name of Allah must be mentioned while the animal is slaughtered, and the blood, which is considered unclean, must be allowed to drain away. Muslims do not eat pork, because they believe that it is unclean.

Alcohol is forbidden, because drunkenness makes people forget that they have duties to Allah, such as prayer.

The spread of Islam

After Muhammad's death, Islam was led by a succession of caliphs (caliph means successor). The first of these was Muhammad's friend, Abu Bakr, and the fourth was his cousin and son-in-law, Ali.

The caliphs waged many wars with the aim both of defending Islam and spreading it. People in conquered countries were supposed to be allowed to keep their religion but had to pay extra taxes, as they were excused from zakah (see page 40) and from military service.

This map shows how far Islam spread in just over 100 years following Muhammad's death. In 661 the center of Islam moved from Mecca to Damascus in Syria and in 750 it moved from Damascus to Baghdad in Iraq, where it remained for the next 500 years.

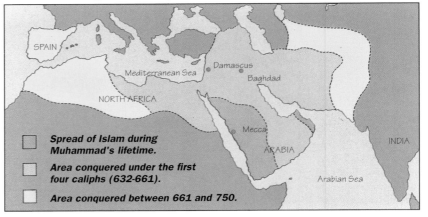

☐ **Spread of Islam during Muhammad's lifetime.**

☐ **Area conquered under the first four caliphs (632-661).**

☐ **Area conquered between 661 and 750.**

Muslim scholarship

Mathematics and science, including medicine and astronomy, as well as art, all flourished in the Muslim world, especially between about 900 and 1200.

In Baghdad a "house of wisdom" was built; this was a great library in which the caliph (see above) wanted to collect copies of all the books in the world.

It was Muslim scholars who introduced many of the works and ideas of the Ancient Greeks and Persians to Europeans. They

A perpetual-motion machine described in a book on waterwheels, which was written in the heyday of Muslim scholarship.

7=VII

Arabic numeral (left) and Roman numerals used previously.

also adopted and established the decimal system of numbers and the concept of zero from India.

The Muslims in Spain

The Muslims conquered much of Spain and Portugal in the 8th century and ruled there right up until the late 15th century, when Spain and Portugal joined forces to overthrow them.

Muslim, Jewish and Christian scholars were all active in Spain at this time. As early as the 10th century, the town of Córdoba had 70 libraries.

A courtyard in the Alhambra, a Muslim palace, at Granada in Spain.

Later Islamic empires

In the 16th and 17th centuries three powerful Islamic empires were at their height. They were all renowned for the splendor of their rulers' courts.

The Ottoman Empire lasted the longest of the three, from the 14th century right up until 1923. It first spread outward from what is now Turkey. By the end of the 15th century, the Muslims had conquered most of the Christian Byzantine world including Constantinople, which they renamed Istanbul.

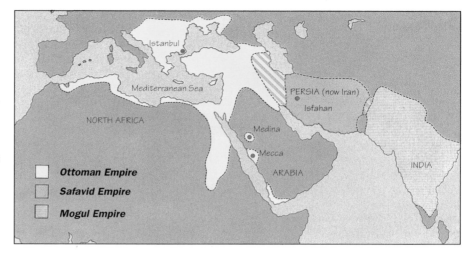

This map shows the three Islamic empires.

Ottoman Empire

Safavid Empire

Mogul Empire

The Shari'ah

The religious laws of Islam are called the Shari'ah, which means the clear, straight path. The sources for the Shari'ah are the Koran and the Sunnah. The Shari'ah gives comprehensive guidelines on matters ranging from personal behavior to conducting matters of state.

In strongly Muslim countries such as Saudi Arabia and Iran, there is little difference between religious laws and the laws of the country. In general, Islam has strict prohibitions and penalties for crimes which are seen to threaten society. The Shari'ah calls for the death penalty for crimes such as murder.

Muslims living in non-Muslim countries are sometimes torn between the need to conform to the laws and customs of the country and the desire to follow the rules of Islam as the Koran dictates. For example, school sports uniforms of shorts or leotards can threaten the Islamic dress code and the publication of books considered blasphemous (which treat Allah with disrespect) can cause offense.

Muslim girls sometimes wear tracksuit trousers under their sports skirts.

Sunni and Shi'ah Islam

About 90 percent of the world's Muslims are known as Sunni Muslims. Sunni means "the path shown by Muhammad".

Shi'ah religious leaders holding a meeting.

Although a much smaller movement than the Sunni, Shi'ah or Shi'ite Islam is dominant in Iran and exists in many other Muslim countries, including southern Iraq, Lebanon and Bahrain.

The main difference between the Sunni and Shi'ah traditions is that Shi'ism does not recognize the first three caliphs and sees the fourth, Ali, as Muhammad's first true successor.

Leaders of Shi'ism in Iran are called ayatollahs, which means "a sign of Allah".

Sufism

Sufi Islam stresses more the idea of a personal relationship with God and less the laws of Islam. Sufi worship includes music, chanting and dancing. Sufi dancers are sometimes known as whirling dervishes. Dervish means wandering beggar: the first Sufis were holy men who lived without possessions.

Whirling dervishes in Turkey.

SIKHISM

Followers of Sikhism are called Sikhs, which means disciples. The religion was founded about 500 years ago, in about 1500, by a man called Nanak. He was known as Guru Nanak. Guru means teacher.

There are about 12 million Sikhs in the world today, mainly in the Punjab region, which is where Sikhism first began.

The Punjab

The Punjab was on the main route into India taken by Muslim invaders in the 15th century. It is a fertile, agricultural region (Punjab means five rivers) and some of the invaders settled there. At the time of Guru Nanak, Hindus and Muslims were living side by side.

The Muslim invaders, who were called Moguls, went on to rule over the whole of northwest India until the 19th century, when the British took over.

In 1947, when India became independent of British rule, the new country of Pakistan was formed in response to demands from Muslims for their own homeland. The Punjab was divided between mainly Hindu India and Muslim Pakistan, and Sikhs who found themselves living in Pakistan had to leave their homes and move to India or countries elsewhere.

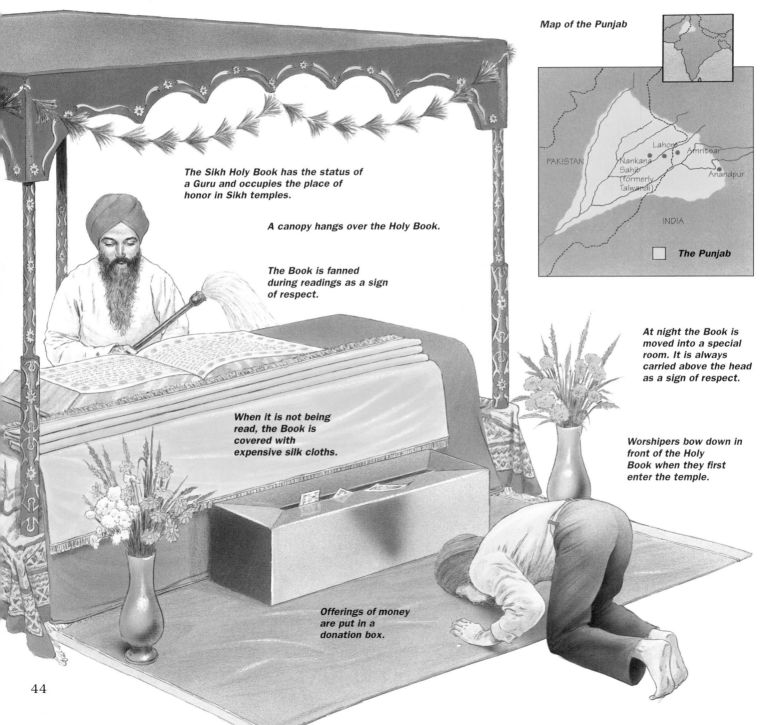

Map of the Punjab

PAKISTAN

Lahore
Nankana
Sahib
(formerly
Talwandi)
Amritsar
Anandpur

INDIA

☐ **The Punjab**

The Sikh Holy Book has the status of a Guru and occupies the place of honor in Sikh temples.

A canopy hangs over the Holy Book.

The Book is fanned during readings as a sign of respect.

At night the Book is moved into a special room. It is always carried above the head as a sign of respect.

When it is not being read, the Book is covered with expensive silk cloths.

Worshipers bow down in front of the Holy Book when they first enter the temple.

Offerings of money are put in a donation box.

44

The Sikh Golden Temple at Amritsar is in the heart of the Punjab region.

Guru Nanak

Nanak was born in 1469 in the village of Talwandi, near Lahore, in the Punjab. His parents were Hindus and he was also used to living alongside and working with Muslims.

When he was 30 years old, Nanak disappeared and was thought to be dead. After a few days he returned and the first words he spoke to

Guru Nanak

anyone were: "There is neither Hindu nor Muslim, so whose path shall I follow? I shall follow God's path." By this he meant that the truth of religion was one and the same, whatever a person's faith. The outward differences between religions are unimportant in God's eyes.

Nanak spent the rest of his life as a wandering teacher, often explaining his ideas in stories.

He is said to have made a point of traveling to both Hindu and Muslim holy places, and he adopted a style of dress which meant that he could not easily be identified either as a Hindu or as a Muslim.

One legend about Nanak describes a disagreement among his followers about his death. The Hindus wanted to cremate his body according to their custom while the Muslims wanted to bury him. When the time came to dispose of the body, the followers found that it had vanished into thin air; only the covering sheet remained.

Equality

Nanak stressed the equality of everyone in God's eyes. He taught that the caste system in India, which put some groups of people above others, was wrong. A story illustrates Nanak's thinking on equality.

On a visit to a village, Nanak refused an invitation to dine with a rich merchant, choosing instead to visit a poor man called Lalo. The rich man was furious. To explain himself, Nanak went to the rich man's house, where he took a handful of bread from the table and squeezed it. Drops of blood spurted out. He then squeezed a lump of bread he had brought

from Lalo's house and pure milk ran out. Nanak explained that although Lalo was poor he was honest, while the rich man's luxury was gained by causing suffering to others.

Nanak's successors

When Nanak was close to death, he chose one of his followers to be his successor. For almost 200 years, Sikh beliefs continued to be passed down through a chain of Gurus.

The ten Gurus

1. Nanak 1469-1539.

2. Angad 1504-1552: he developed a written script for the Punjabi language (Gurmukhi).

This painting shows an imaginary meeting between Guru Nanak and the nine other Gurus. Guru Nanak is being fanned by a servant. The man in the middle at the front is a musician.

3. Amar Das 1479-1574.

4. Ram Das 1534-1581: he founded the holy city of Amritsar.

5. Arjan 1563-1606: he built the Golden Temple at Amritsar.

6. Har Gobind 1595-1645: the first "warrior Guru"; he led Sikh resistance against the Muslim Mogul rulers.

7. Har Rai 1630-1661.

8. Har Krishan 1656-1664.

9. Tegh Bahadur 1621-1675.

10. Gobind Singh 1666-1708: he founded the Sikh brotherhood, the Khalsa (see next page).

The Khalsa

From time to time, Sikhs suffered persecution at the hands of certain of the Muslim Mogul rulers of India. The fifth and ninth Gurus were both put to death for their beliefs.

The tenth Guru, Gobind Singh, decided to found the Khalsa (brotherhood). This was to be a group of devoted Sikhs who were prepared to resist oppression and defend their faith, by the sword if necessary.

During a festival in 1699, Gobind Singh summoned his followers to Anandpur. When they arrived, they found their Guru standing outside a large tent with his sword drawn. He asked for volunteers who were ready to die for the Sikh faith. Eventually, a man stepped forward and was led into the tent. The crowd heard a sickening thud and Gobind Singh reappeared with his sword covered in blood. Despite the terror of most of the crowd, this procedure was repeated again and again. When a fifth volunteer had entered the tent, the Guru reappeared: with all five men alive and well.

They were dressed in yellow robes and declared to be Panj Piare, the Beloved Five. These five brave men were the first members of the new brotherhood.

The Amrit ceremony

The five volunteers were baptized with a mixture of sugar and water, amrit, which they drank from the same bowl and had sprinkled on their heads. The Guru was also baptized to show equality within the Khalsa.

The crowd was inspired by their example, and thousands became baptized Sikhs with full membership of the Khalsa.

Sikhs of both sexes can still choose to join the brotherhood; if they do, they take part in an Amrit ceremony presided over by five outstanding members of the community who represent the original Beloved Five.

A woman at her Amrit ceremony.

When Sikhs join the Khalsa, they take a new name. Men are known as Singh, which means lion, and women take the name Kaur, which means princess. Originally, the new names were intended to promote equality by removing any traces of caste indicated by people's names.

Beliefs

Sikhs believe in one God, who should be worshiped by living honestly and caring for others. Sikhs do not use images in their worship as this might encourage superstition. They aim to lead disciplined lives and to work in jobs which benefit society. They are not allowed to smoke or drink alcohol. Devoted Sikhs begin each day at dawn by washing and reflecting on the teachings of the Gurus.

Service

Service to others, which is called sewa, is thought to bring people closer to God. As well as offering practical help, Sikhs are expected to give a tenth of their income to others. This social service is usually organized through temples.

Helping with building work on temples is a way of performing sewa.

The five Ks

Guru Gobind Singh gave the brotherhood a distinctive uniform. Each part of the uniform begins with the letter K in Punjabi, so they are known as the five Ks. Many Sikhs, whether they are baptized or unbaptized, wear the five Ks today.

Kesh - Uncut hair. This shows obedience to God's will by interfering with nature as little as possible. A turban is worn, usually by men, to keep the long hair neat.

(Boys who are not yet old enough to join the Khalsa but who are growing their hair in preparation cover it with a small cloth like this.)

Kangha - Wooden comb. The long hair must be kept neat, and not allowed to become matted like that of some holy men.

Kachera - White shorts, to be worn under clothes. These symbolize purity and modesty, and were practical for people who might have to fight.

Kara - Steel bangle. The circle represents eternity; the steel: strength and purity. Worn on the right arm, the sword arm, it is a reminder to fight only for God.

Kirpan - Short sword. A reminder to defend truth and what is right. Today, symbolic kirpan brooches are often worn instead of the short sword itself.

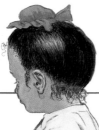

The Holy Book

The last Guru, Gobind Singh, decided that nobody was worthy to become his successor and that to select someone would, in any case, go against the principles of equality which he had tried to promote through the Khalsa.

In future, the Sikh scriptures were to be the Guru and guide Sikhism's followers. The scriptures are called the Guru Granth Sahib and are treated with the greatest respect. They consist mainly of hymns written by the Gurus, expressing Sikh beliefs. Also included are writings by both Hindus and Muslims.

A page from the Guru Granth Sahib.

The gurdwara

A Sikh temple is called a gurdwara, which means "door to the Guru".

Anyone entering the gurdwara must cover their head and take off their shoes. They wash before entering the prayer room.

Everyone sits on the floor and only the Guru Granth Sahib is raised above others. Although men and women usually sit separately, women have always been regarded as equal in worship. They can read from the Holy Book and so lead the service. There are no priests.

After the final prayer, karah parshad is distributed among the worshipers. This is a mixture of sugar, butter and flour which has been stirred with a kirpan.

A yellow flag showing the symbol of Sikhism is flown outside temples.

The circle on the flag, with no beginning and no end, represents eternity. It also stands for the unity of all Sikhs.

The crossed daggers are a reminder to Sikhs to be prepared to defend their faith.

The double-edged sword represents the power of truth.

The langar

Every temple has a dining room, called a langar. Food and money given by worshipers are used to provide a communal meal after the service. The temple will provide a meal and a place to sleep for anyone who needs it.

Preparing food in the langar.

Music plays an important part in services in the gurdwara.

The gurdwara is an important center for the Sikh community as well as a place of worship. It contains meeting rooms and classrooms, where Sikh children living outside the Punjab have lessons in Punjabi.

Festivals

Sikhs keep some of the same festivals as Hindus. Divali, for example, is celebrated as a festival of lights. For Sikhs it is also a reminder of Guru Har Gobind, imprisoned by a Mogul emperor and released at Divali.

The Baisakhi festival, held in April, is both a New Year festival and a reminder of the founding of the Khalsa. On the third day, the flagpole outside the gurdwara is given a new flag.

Gurpurbs are festivals which mark the birthdays or deaths of the Gurus. Two important gurpurbs are those of Guru Nanak in November and Guru Gobind Singh in December or January. The gurpurb consists of processions and shared celebratory meals. The Guru Granth Sahib plays an important role and is often carried through the streets.

Boys taking part in the gurpurb of Guru Gobind Singh.

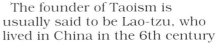

SOME OTHER RELIGIONS

On the next four pages you can find out about some other religions which have not yet been dealt with in this book. Although they do not have as many followers as the religions already described, they are very important in those areas where they are practiced, and for the influence they have had on cultures elsewhere.

Shinto

Shinto, which means "the Way of the Gods", is a Japanese religion, practiced today by around five million people. Its roots date back to at least 1000BC.

The religion is based on the belief that spiritual powers exist in the natural world, for example in trees, the wind, stones, animals and people, including the dead. These powers, or gods, are called kami.

The decorated box in this photograph is said to contain a kami. It is about to be paraded by priests at a festival.

Shinto places of worship are often situated in beautiful natural settings. Each one is the home of a particular kami.

Mount Fuji in Japan is sacred to the goddess Amaterasu (see page 8). People make pilgrimages to climb it.

Buildings of worship are called shrines. The inner hall, where the kami is thought to be present, is entered only by priests. The idea of purity is important in Shinto and worshipers rinse their mouth and wash their hands before they enter the prayer hall.

The entrance to a Shinto shrine is always marked by an archway called a torii.

Worship takes place at home and in work places too. Offerings of rice and tea are made at a special shelf, called a godshelf, and prayers are said, often to the family ancestors.

Many people in Japan practice both Shinto and Buddhism. It is quite common to have a Shinto wedding but a Buddhist funeral.

Taoism

Tao, pronounced "dow", is often translated as "the Way". To Taoists, this is the ultimate reality or underlying spiritual force of the universe, which is present in all things, yet greater than all things. The goal of Taoists is to become merged with the Way and so achieve liberation and become one of the Immortals.

The Tao is in a constant state of flux, so the Taoist must learn to tune into this endlessly changing flow of life and penetrate its secret. The way to learn to "go with the flow" is through meditation and contemplation.

T'ai Chi Ch'uan, practiced by millions of Chinese, is thought to have been devised by a Taoist priest. It consists of sequences of very slow, controlled movements and is a form of meditation.

The founder of Taoism is usually said to be Lao-tzu, who lived in China in the 6th century BC. However, some modern scholars think that neither he nor his successor, Chuang-tzu, actually existed.

Lao-tzu, as shown in a sculpture. According to a legend, he rode on an ox.

Although religion is not officially allowed in Communist China, Taoism is still practiced there and in other Far Eastern countries (see map opposite) by about five million people, often in conjunction with Confucianism and Buddhism.

This Taoist symbol represents the harmonious interaction of the two opposing forces of the universe: yin (male) and yang (female).

Confucianism

Confucianism takes its name from the Chinese philosopher, Confucius, who lived in the 6th century BC. His name was really K'ung Fu-tzu; Confucius is the Westernized version.

The writings of Confucius were originally intended as advice for the rulers of China. Confucius emphasized the dignity of humanity and the importance of people behaving appropriately to their position in life. He thought that society could become perfect, if its members worked hard to achieve "beautiful conduct". This involves always being considerate to others, respecting ancestors and aiming for harmony and balance in all things, avoiding extremes of emotion and behavior. If people live in peace and harmony, they will be in contact with the spiritual forces of the universe, including those of nature.

A Confucian ceremony in Seoul, South Korea, in which people come together to pay respect to their ancestors.

A modern statue of Confucius in Singapore.

It has sometimes been said that Confucianism is not really a religion because it puts more emphasis on becoming a good citizen than on spirituality. However, Confucius said, "Heaven is the author of the virtue that is in me," and he saw heaven as a kind of supreme being.

The teachings of Confucius were developed by his followers and gradually acquired elements of both Buddhism and Taoism. Today, Confucianism is practiced by about five million people in China and the Far East.

Map of South and East Asia, showing areas where Confucianism and Taoism are practiced today. These religions have also influenced the practice of Buddhism in nearby countries such as Japan.

South China Sea

■ Confucianism
□ Taoism

Jainism

The most important figure in the history of Jainism is a man called Mahavira, who lived in India in the 6th century BC. He was a contemporary of the Buddha and is mentioned in Buddhist scriptures. Jains share many beliefs with both Hindus and Buddhists. They believe in karma and rebirth, and seek release from the cycle of existence (see page 13).

According to Jainism, the way to seek release is to show the greatest respect for all forms of life and harm no living thing. Jains are very strict vegetarians and will not even eat root vegetables because the whole plant dies when its root is pulled up.

Jainism teaches that people should have as few possessions as possible because happiness can never come from material things. The religion requires great self-discipline and many of its followers are monks and nuns (see page 6).

Mahavira was said to be the 24th in a chain of great spiritual teachers called Tirthankaras (Pathmakers). Jain temples contain statues of the 24.

People who achieve release are called jinas, which means "those who overcome". The religion takes its name from them.

Jains believe in the individual soul but not in any kind of supreme being. For them, the universe is without beginning or end, so they do not need to believe in a creator. Today there are about three million Jains, mainly in western India.

Jain monks used to retreat to the mountains, forests or caves to fast and meditate close to nature. They had so few possessions, they did not even wear clothes.

49

Zoroastrianism

Zoroastrianism was founded by a prophet of ancient Persia (now Iran). He was called Zarathustra or Zoroaster. He is traditionally thought to have lived around 600BC but some experts think it was much earlier, around 1500BC.

Zoroaster, holding a fire symbol. Fire is sacred to Zoroastrians and a flame is always kept burning in temples.

Followers of Zoroastrianism are called Parsis, which originally meant Persian. They were given this name at the end of the 9th century AD, when many of them left Persia because they were being persecuted by the Muslim rulers. They went to the Bombay area of India, which is where most of today's 150,000 Parsis still live.

According to Zoroaster, the world, which was originally perfect, became the battleground for a struggle between the forces of good and the forces of evil. God (Ahura Mazda) is the origin of all that is good, while evil comes from the Destructive Spirit (Angra Mainyu). People have to choose between good and evil. Those who live good, simple lives will go to heaven and be united with God; those who choose evil will go to hell.

Angra Mainyu

Zoroaster predicted that one day the battle would end and the world would be restored to perfection again.

Purity is of great importance in Zoroastrianism and any form of decay, such as rust, should be avoided. Death, with its bodily decay, is seen as the temporary victory of evil.

The earth must not be contaminated by having the dead buried in it and cremation is not possible because fire is sacred. The dead must be kept separate from the living. For these reasons, whenever possible, Parsis put their dead at the top of "towers of silence" and let birds of prey devour the flesh, while they pray in a nearby building. The bones are later put in a pit.

A tower of silence in India.

Baha'ism

This is a new faith which began in Persia (now Iran) in the 19th century. A man called Mirza Ali Muhammad, who was known as the Bab ("gate" to the truth) predicted that a great prophet would come after him. That prophet is thought to be a man known as Baha'u'llah, which means Glory of God. He lived from 1817 to 1892. Baha'is see him as the latest and most important in a line of prophets which includes Adam, Moses, Krishna, Buddha, Zoroaster, Christ and Muhammad.

Baha'u'llah saw himself as a savior and believed that it was God's will that he and his followers should try to unite humanity by bringing all the faiths of the world into harmony. Then there could be a new world age, with peace, justice and an end to religious and racial prejudice.

The symbol of Baha'ism is a nine-pointed star.

The Most Holy Book contains the laws of Baha'u'llah and covers all aspects of behavior, both private and public. Baha'i laws include obligatory prayer, fasting and avoidance of alcohol. Marriage is very much encouraged. Today, the laws and issues such as world unity are debated at conferences, when Baha'is from many different religious and cultural backgrounds all meet together.

Baha'is in Iran have suffered from persecution from the Muslim rulers. Members of the faith now live all over the world and their numbers have grown to over three million. The headquarters of Baha'ism are at Haifa in Israel, where the Bab is buried and which Baha'u'llah visited several times. It is a place of pilgrimage.

The temple at Haifa, in Israel, which contains the tomb of the Bab.

50

Rastafarianism

Rastafarianism is a very recent religion, founded in the 1930s. Marcus Garvey, a Jamaican, predicted that there would be a black messiah in Africa. When Ras (Prince) Tafari came to the throne of Ethiopia in 1930 as Emperor Haile Selassie, he was hailed as this messiah.

Haile Selassie

Rastafarians (or Rastas for short) accept some of the teachings of the Bible because that is the tradition of Ethiopia. They believe God took human form, first as Christ, then as Ras Tafari. They liken the fate of all black people in the West to that of the Israelites enslaved in Egypt and Babylon, and believe that they will not be free unless they return to Africa. This is now understood by many Rastas as a spiritual state of mind rather than the actual place.

Rastas try to live as close to nature as possible. Ideally they would grow their own food and many are vegetarian, do not smoke tobacco or drink alcohol or coffee. They have often come into conflict with the law, however, because of their use of the drug cannabis.

Many Rastas wear their hair in a style known as dreadlocks. They do not cut it or comb it.

The hairstyle is similar to that of ancient African priests and some Israelites.

They consider this a natural and beneficial herb, and many smoke it as part of their worship.

Rastafarianism is strongest in Jamaica but has spread to other Afro-Caribbean communities, particularly in the USA and Europe. Young people especially respond to the positive image of blackness and the message of freedom. There are over 100,000 Rastas.

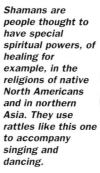

Rastas often wear hats in the colors of the Ethiopian flag.

Music is an important part of worship and reggae was developed by Rastafarian musicians.

Local religions

There are many other religions not mentioned in this book. Many of these are practiced in specific, local areas and so tend to have smaller numbers of followers than other religions. Many of these local religions have no written scriptures and beliefs are passed on by word of mouth from generation to generation.

The parts of the world where most of the local religions are found include North and South America (among native American peoples); Australia (among, for example, the Aboriginal and Maori peoples); Arctic regions such as Siberia and Alaska; and Africa.

Local religions have often come under threat from other, more powerful societies. Some have been destroyed completely, while many have been influenced and changed by other faiths. On the other hand, local religions can also influence the way in which major religions are practiced. In Africa, for instance, local religions influence Christianity and Islam as well as vice versa.

Bark paintings by Australian Aborigines record the history and beliefs of their religion and are considered sacred. Animals and the natural world are of great importance to the Aborigines.

Sedna is a goddess of the Inuit people of the Arctic. If they do not behave correctly towards nature, Sedna will prevent their hunters from finding the animals they need to survive.

Shamans are people thought to have special spiritual powers, of healing for example, in the religions of native North Americans and in northern Asia. They use rattles like this one to accompany singing and dancing.

MAP OF RELIGIONS

This map shows the main religions of different parts of the world. The main religion is the one which has a clear majority of an area's population claiming to be followers*. It does not mean that it is necessarily the official state religion.

Stripes indicate that no one religion has a clear majority of the region's population and that another faith has roughly equal numbers of followers.

In addition to the religions shown in a country, there may be many others that are practiced there. For instance, although the majority of people in India are Hindu, there are several other

Christianity

Catholic

Protestant

Orthodox

Islam

Sunni

Shi'ah

Buddhism

Mahayana

Theravada

Hinduism

Judaism

Sikhism

Shinto

Confucianism

Local religions

State atheism

52

*See page 3 for an explanation of how religious believers are counted.

religions there too. Also, the influence of local religions is often greater than it appears from statistics, especially in Africa and South America.

Religions are not confined to areas where they are shown on the map. For example, Israel is the only country with Judaism as its main religion, yet only about a quarter of the world's Jews live in Israel.

The numbers of people living in different parts of the world vary enormously, so large expanses of one religion on this map do not necessarily mean large numbers of followers. Areas of low population include those on the northern edges of the map, northern and central Australia and the Sahara desert in North Africa.

RELIGIONS OF THE PAST

Many religions which used to be practiced no longer exist today. Some died out because the societies which practiced them died out. Others died out because people were converted to other religions. Most of what is known about these ancient religions has been worked out from archeologists' finds.

This statue was unearthed in Austria. It is about 22,000 years old and is thought to be of a fertility goddess.

Although ancient religions were extremely varied, many had similarities. For example, all the religions mentioned on these two pages involved the worship of many gods and goddesses. These were often aspects of nature such as the sky or water, plants or animals. They could also represent abstract qualities such as truth or beauty, activities such as farming, the seasons and places.

Re, the sun god of the Ancient Egyptians.

Although the gods and goddesses were considered immortal, they were often thought of as having human personalities and feelings, and near-human lifestyles. Worship involved trying to please them and avoid their anger, by making offerings of food, for instance, or sacrificing animals and, in some cases, even human beings. Disasters such as illness, floods or war were often seen as punishments from the gods.

Many of these "dead" religions have had a great influence on modern culture, featuring, for example, in art and literature.

This 16th century painting shows Phaethon, son of the Greek sun god. According to legend, he drove his father's chariot without permission and tipped it over, almost setting the world on fire.

The earliest religions

Much about very early religions remains a mystery and, as they existed before writing did, there are no historical documents about them. Archeologists have found objects that are thought to be religious, dating back to 35,000BC or even earlier.

In Europe, between about 5000 and 2000BC, monuments made of huge stones called megaliths were erected. Getting the stones into position was a mammoth task. Some of these monuments were used for religious ceremonies.

Stonehenge, a megalithic monument in England.

In many places it was common for people to be buried with some of their belongings. Were these for use in an afterlife?

This man was buried in England in about 2000BC.

Dagger

Drinking pot

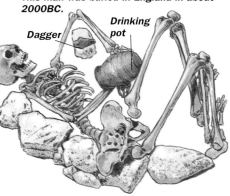

Mesopotamia (c.3500BC-100AD)

Mesopotamia corresponded roughly with modern Iraq. Its religion is one of the oldest that is known about in any detail. This is because writing was first developed in Mesopotamia in about 3500BC, so there are records of beliefs and practices.

A Mesopotamian ziggurat: a stepped platform with a temple on top.

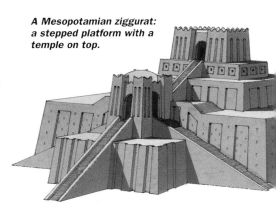

The story of the Flood, described in both Jewish and Christian scriptures, is thought by some experts to have originated in Mesopotamia centuries earlier.

The Egyptians (c.3000-30BC)

The Egyptians had a strong belief in a joyful life after death for those who had lived good lives. For a person's three souls to function properly, it was thought essential for their body to be preserved from decay. This is why bodies were mummified in Ancient Egypt.

A mummy with objects needed for life in the Next World. The objects are a wine jar (with handles), an oil jar and a box of clothes.

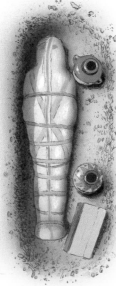

In the first century AD, Christianity became popular in Egypt and traditional beliefs waned. Later, in 641, a Muslim invasion converted the country to Islam, which is still its main religion today.

The Greeks (c.750-30BC)

The Ancient Greek gods and goddesses were thought to live on the highest Greek mountain, Mount Olympus, where they had many love affairs. The king of the gods was Zeus, controller of the sky and of thunder.

A statue of Zeus, about to throw a thunderbolt.

The Greeks believed that after death a person's soul went to the Underworld, where its fate was judged according to the life the person had led. Very virtuous souls were sent to the Elysian Fields, a happy place full of sunshine.

The Romans
(c.500BC-400AD)

As the Romans expanded beyond Rome, they came into contact with people of several different religions. They often added the gods of these religions to their own. In particular, they matched their Roman gods to the Greek gods. Jupiter, chief Roman god, is the equivalent of Zeus.

All the planets in the solar system, except Earth, are named after Roman gods.

This statue shows the Greek and Roman goddess of hunting: Artemis (Greek) or Diana (Roman).

Germanic and Norse religions (c.700-1000)

The religion of the Germanic and Norse (Scandinavian) peoples had periods of popularity all over Europe before the area became Christian. It was spread by the Vikings (Norse seamen) among others.

The English words for some of the days of the week come from Germanic and Norse gods, for example: Tuesday from Tiw, the god of war; Wednesday from Woden, the chief god; Thursday from Thor, the god of thunder; and Friday from Frigg or Freyja, the goddess of love and death.

Odin, Woden or Wotan, the chief Germanic and Norse god, on his eight-legged horse.

America before Columbus

Several religions had been practiced in Central and South America before it was Christianized by the Spanish, who sent explorers such as Christopher Columbus there in the late 15th century.

Map showing the location of the great Mayan, Aztec and Inca Empires.

A sun festival commemorating the Incas is still held in Peru. Worship of the sun god was central to the Inca religion.

The man being carried is dressed as the sun god.

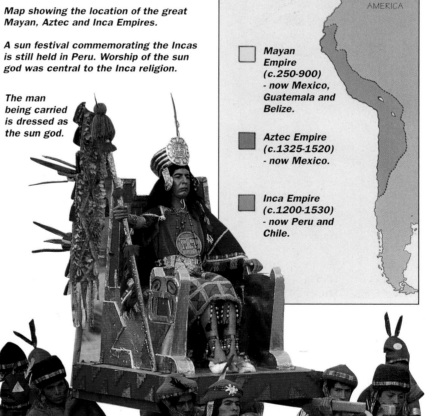

CENTRAL AMERICA

Pacific Ocean

SOUTH AMERICA

☐ **Mayan Empire (c.250-900)** - now Mexico, Guatemala and Belize.

■ **Aztec Empire (c.1325-1520)** - now Mexico.

■ **Inca Empire (c.1200-1530)** - now Peru and Chile.

TIME CHART OF RELIGIONS

This time chart will help you see at a glance when most of the major religions in the world first began. Many of the starting dates are approximate and broken lines indicate that nobody really knows quite how far back the religion goes. The front edge of the chart shows the present day.

Local religions go back much further than the earliest date shown on this chart. Evidence has been found of religious belief dating back to 35,000BC.

Religions which have died out are all shown in pale blue. You can see that these are not necessarily very ancient. The Inca and Aztec religions, for example, were relatively recent, looked at on the time scale of this chart. They did, however, incorporate many beliefs of much earlier peoples.

The panels down the right-hand edge of the chart show a few key events in the history of different religions.

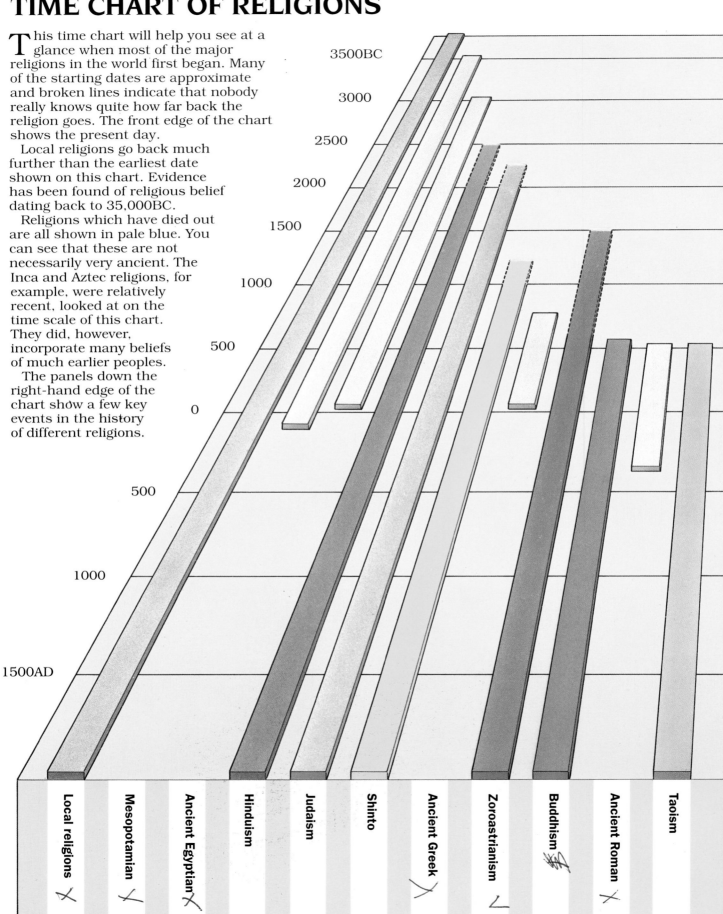

3500BC
3000
2500
2000
1500
1000
500
0
500
1000
1500AD

Local religions
Mesopotamian
Ancient Egyptian
Hinduism
Judaism
Shinto
Ancient Greek
Zoroastrianism
Buddhism
Ancient Roman
Taoism

56

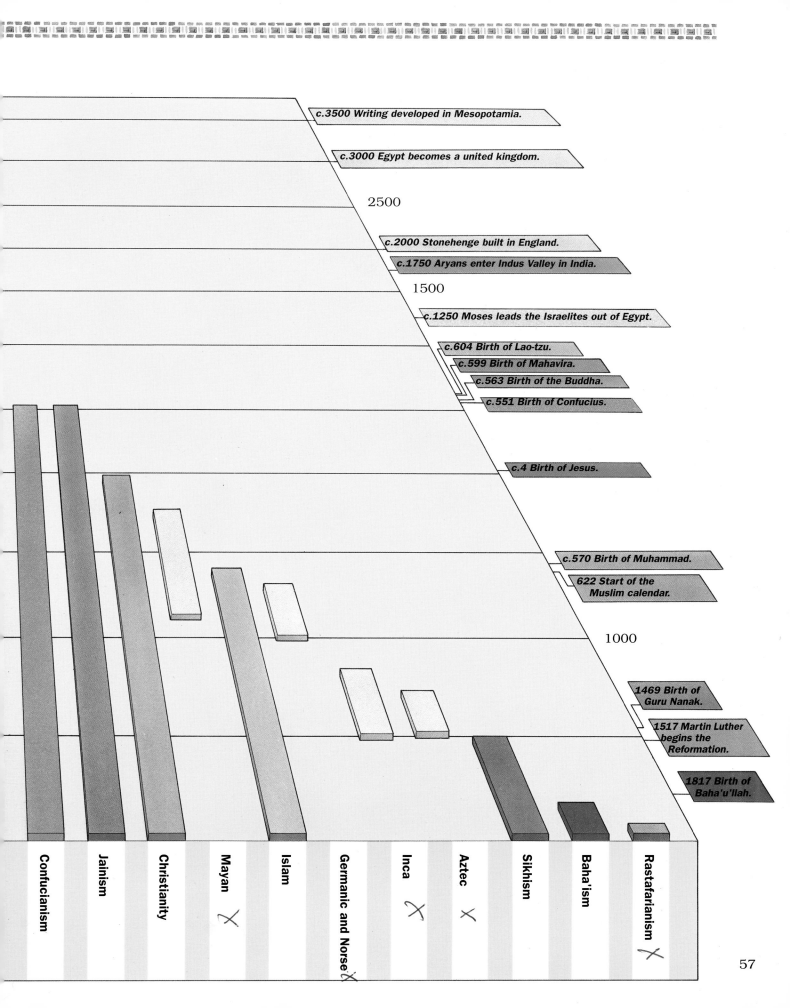

c.3500 Writing developed in Mesopotamia.

c.3000 Egypt becomes a united kingdom.

2500

c.2000 Stonehenge built in England.

c.1750 Aryans enter Indus Valley in India.

1500

c.1250 Moses leads the Israelites out of Egypt.

c.604 Birth of Lao-tzu.

c.599 Birth of Mahavira.

c.563 Birth of the Buddha.

c.551 Birth of Confucius.

c.4 Birth of Jesus.

c.570 Birth of Muhammad.

622 Start of the Muslim calendar.

1000

1469 Birth of Guru Nanak.

1517 Martin Luther begins the Reformation.

1817 Birth of Baha'u'llah.

Confucianism
Jainism
Christianity
Mayan
Islam
Germanic and Norse
Inca
Aztec
Sikhism
Baha'ism
Rastafarianism

57

NONCONFORMIST GROUPS

Most of the groups listed here grew out of the Protestant, Nonconformist movement in Christianity (see page 34). Some have tens of millions of members. A few of the groups do not regard themselves as Christians. A few are not considered to be Christians by other groups.

The paragraphs in boxes explain some general ideas held by several of the different groups listed.

Baptists

The Baptist Church began in the early 17th century in Britain and is now one of the largest Protestant Churches, with members all over the world.

Baptists practice "believers' baptism" and so do not baptize babies and children because they are not old enough to understand the significance of the ceremony. Baptism involves full immersion in the water.

Baptists stress the importance of the teachings of the Bible as well as personal faith in Christ.

A woman being baptized into the Baptist Church.

Christian Scientists

Christian Scientists believe there is a law of God working only for good, which can be applied in all situations to bring about right ideas, right action and healing. Christian Science was founded in 1879 in America by Mary Baker Eddy, as a church designed to carry the message of God's healing power, as demonstrated by Jesus, into the world.

Church of Christ

Members of the Church of Christ, found mainly in the USA, believe in following strictly the teachings of the New Testament (see page 32) and reject all other traditions and creeds. They are very similar to another, smaller group called the Disciples of Christ.

The second coming

This is described in the Bible as the time when Christ will come again. Then, the Day of Judgment will take place: both the living and the dead will be judged on their deeds and their faith, and God's kingdom (see page 31) will be established here on earth.

The second coming is understood very differently by different Christians. A few take it literally, believing that people will be sent either to heaven or hell after being judged; many believe that God's kingdom will be for all Christians or even for all humanity; some think that the second coming describes the hopes of human beings for a better spiritual life in general.

Congregationalists

Each Congregational Church is independent and governs itself. This means that the beliefs of Congregationalists can be diverse. However, they are similar to those of the Presbyterians (see opposite page). Congregationalism, which began in the 16th century, is popular in the USA, Eastern Europe and Britain.

Holiness Movement

There are many different types of Churches in the Holiness Movement but all are dedicated to striving for human perfection through following Christianity. This movement rejects the materialistic values of modern society and stresses the importance of the spiritual life. The largest Holiness Church is the Church of the Nazarene.

Jehovah's Witnesses

Jehovah's Witnesses believe that the second coming of Christ (see above) will be very soon, when only the faithful will be saved. They feel it is their duty to convert others so that they too can repent of their sins and join the faithful; they try to do this by preaching from house to house.

Witnesses have strict rules for living. They do not celebrate birthdays or festivals such as Christmas and Easter. They do not accept blood transfusions, are pacifist and will not take part in politics. All these rules are based on their own interpretation of the Bible.

The Witnesses do not believe in the Trinity (see page 33) and are opposed to the established Churches. They meet in halls known as Kingdom Halls.

The movement was founded in America in the 1870s by Charles Taze Russell. Jehovah is the name for God in the Old Testament (see page 32).

Lutherans

The Lutheran Church is based on the ideas of Martin Luther (see page 34). It is one of the largest Protestant Churches in the world, and is the state Church in Germany and most Scandinavian countries.

A Lutheran church

Mennonites

Named after their Dutch founder in the 16th century, Menno Simons, most Mennonites today are found in America and Canada. They practice "believers' baptism" (See "Baptists" above) and have similar ideas to the Amish (see page 9).

Methodists (see page 34)

Mormons

Members of the Church of Jesus Christ of Latter-day Saints believe that their faith is a restoration of the original Christian Church, complete with living apostles and a living prophet, new scripture and continuous revelation. They believe that all human beings are literally children of a Heavenly Father and have equal potential for eternal progression.

Latter-day Saints only baptize children of eight and over, who are considered old enough to be accountable for their actions. Latter-day Saints can be baptized on behalf of their dead ancestors. They believe that marriage is for eternity.

The faith was founded in America in 1830. Believers accept the Book of Mormon, a religious account of an ancient American civilization, as a companion scripture to the Bible. It is from that book that Latter-day Saints gained the nickname, Mormons.

Pentecostalists

The Pentecostal Movement began in America at the beginning of the 20th century and is the fastest-growing branch of Christianity today. Its members attach great importance to the Day of Pentecost (see page 37) and the workings of the Holy Spirit. They believe the Holy Spirit gave the disciples the ability to "speak in tongues", that is, in languages other than their own.

Worship is emotional and spontaneous, depending on how the Holy Spirit moves each individual. People often "speak in tongues" and recount life-changing personal experiences. Pentecostalists believe in faith healing: the healing of illness through the power of people's faith in the Holy Spirit.

The Pentecostalist style of worship has influenced many different types of Churches. Pentecostalists are sometimes known as Charismatics, especially in the Catholic Church.

Pentecostalists worshiping

Evangelicals

This term usually refers to Protestants who have had an intense conversion experience. Such Christians also describe themselves as "born again", because the conversion has led them to a new life "in the spirit".

The word, evangelical, comes from the same root as evangelist (see page 33) and evangelicals are enthusiastic in their efforts to convert others. They stress the importance of the Bible and personal faith in Christ rather than Church rituals.

Presbyterians

Presbyterianism is based on the ideas of John Calvin (see page 34). It is one of the largest Protestant Churches in the world and is found especially in the USA, the Netherlands and Scotland. The Church of Scotland is Presbyterian.

Quakers

The proper name for Quakers is the Society of Friends. The Society was founded in the 17th century in Britain by George Fox. The nickname, Quakers, came from a speech made by Fox, in which he said "You should quake at the word of the Lord".

One of the main Quaker beliefs is that each person has an "inner light" in their soul. For this reason Quakers do not have priests or any rituals such as set prayers in their worship. Worship is mainly silent until someone feels moved by the Holy Spirit to speak. Places of worship are known as Meeting Houses. The Society is known for its pacifism and its charity work.

The American state of Pennsylvania was founded as an experiment in Quaker living by William Penn in 1681.

Salvation Army

The Salvation Army was begun in England in 1865 by William and Catherine Booth. They felt the working classes were not responding to the established Christian Churches because they were too poor and badly educated. The Salvation Army preaches that people should repent of their sins, and they do a lot of charity work, including providing food and shelter for the homeless. They are well-known for their opposition to drinking alcohol.

Salvation Army members hold open-air services and are easily recognized by their uniforms and brass bands.

Seventh Day Adventists

An Adventist is someone who believes that the second coming of Christ is imminent.

Seventh Day Adventists believe in the importance of honoring the Sabbath, which they take to be from sunset on Friday to sunset on Saturday. They stress the importance of the Bible and do not smoke, or drink alcohol.

Unitarians

Some Unitarians consider themselves Christians; some do not. Unitarians believe in the oneness of God and reject the doctrine of the Trinity (see page 33); they do not believe that Jesus was anything other than human. They put a lot of emphasis on reason and science, and campaign for human rights.

United Reformed Church

United Reformed Churches can be a combination of any of the "reformed" Churches which grew out of the Reformation (see page 34). In England and Wales the United Reformed Church consists of the Congregationalists and the Presbyterians, who merged in 1972.

RELIGIOUS SAYINGS

Below are just a few sayings from different religions. The names of the people who said them or the scriptures from which they are taken are given in italics after each one.

Hindu

From the unreal lead me to the real, from darkness lead me to light, from death lead me to immortality. *Brihadaranyaka Upanishad*

As leaving aside worn-out garments A man takes other, new ones, So leaving aside worn-out bodies To other, new ones goes the embodied (soul). *Bhagavad Gita*

Real happiness of heart cannot be attained without giving up the ideas of "I" and "mine". *Tulsidas*

The light of the gas illumines various localities with various intensities. But the life of the light, namely the gas, comes from one common reservoir. So the teachers of all climes and ages are but as many lampposts through which is emitted the light of the spirit flowing constantly from the one source, the Lord Almighty. *Ramakrishna*

Earth has enough for everyone's need but not for everyone's greed. *Mahatma Gandhi*

Jewish

To everything there is a season, and a time to every purpose under the heaven. *Ecclesiastes*

Whether Jew or non-Jew, man or woman, rich or poor, it is according to deeds that God's presence descends. *Talmud*

What is hateful to you, do not do to your neighbor. That is the whole Torah. The rest is commentary. Go and learn it. *Rabbi Hillel*

When God created the first man, He led him all around the trees in the Garden of Eden. God said to him: "See my works, how beautiful and praiseworthy they are. Everything I have created has been created for your sake. Think of this, and do not corrupt it, there will be no one to set it right after you." *Midrash*

Do not limit a child to your own learning, for he was born in another time. *Talmud*

Buddhist

It is you who must make the effort. The Great of the past only showed the way. *Dhammapada*

There are two extremes which should be avoided:
1 Indulgence in sensual pleasures and
2 Indulgence in extreme hardship. *Dhammacakkappavattama Sutra*

It is easy to see the faults of others, but difficult to see one's own faults. One shows the faults of others like chaff winnowed in the wind, but one conceals one's own faults as a cunning gambler conceals his dice. *Dhammapada*

If you are afraid, you are in error. If you know how to calm your spirit and keep it still in all circumstances, you are in truth. *Bodhidharma*

Go forth, O monks, for the good of the many, for the welfare of the many; out of compassion for the world teach this Dhamma which is glorious in the beginning, glorious in the middle and glorious at the end, in the spirit and in the letter. *Vinaya Pitaka*

Christian

For what shall it profit a man, if he shall gain the whole world, and lose his own soul? *Mark's Gospel*

The truth shall make you free. *John's Gospel*

In the beginning was the Word, and the Word was with God, and the Word was God. *John's Gospel*

Blessed are the peacemakers: for they shall be called the children of God. *Matthew's Gospel*

Do all the good you can,
By all the means you can,
In all the ways you can,
At all the times you can,
To all the people you can,
As long as ever you can.
John Wesley

If anyone says "I love God" and hates his brother, he is a liar; for he who does not love his brother whom he has seen, cannot love God whom he has not seen. *John's First Letter*

And now faith, hope and love abide, these three: and the greatest of these is love. *St Paul*

Muslim

In the whole universe of creation there is nothing that is either the like or the equal or the contrary of God. God is Exalted above all form, indeed immune to and free from form. *Ibrahim Haqqi*

Whatever good happens to you is from God; and whatever evil happens to you is from yourself. *Qur'an*

Three things cannot be retrieved:
The arrow once sped from the bow,
The word spoken in haste,
The missed opportunity.
Ali, Caliph of Islam

The best Islam consists in feeding the hungry and in greeting those one knows and those one does not know, too. *Hadith*

Trust in God - but tie your camel first.
Sufi Sayings of Muhammad

Many paths lead to God; I have chosen that of music and dancing. *Rumi, a Sufi mystic*

Sikh

God is the fish and the fisherman, the water and the net, the float of the net and the bait within it. *Guru Nanak*

You are blessed by being born human, it is an opportunity which has been given you to meet your God. *Adi Granth*

Let no one be proud of their birth. Know that we are all born from the same clay. *Guru Nanak*

Just as the poor castor oil plant imbibes the scent of the nearest sandalwood, so wrongdoers become emancipated through the company of the faithful. *Adi Granth*

GLOSSARY

Absolution
In Christianity, Christ's forgiveness of sins, declared by a priest.

Advent
The four weeks during which Christians prepare for Christmas, by remembering Old Testament prophecies about the coming of the Messiah.

Ancestor worship
The practice, especially in Far Eastern and African religions, of honoring ancestors with special rituals. Ancestors are sometimes thought to intervene, for good or ill, in human life.

Angels
Heavenly beings, in Judaism, Christianity and Islam. They often represent different virtues, such as mercy, and act as messengers of God.

Apocalypse
A word used in the Bible for the end of the world.

Apostles
The original 12 disciples chosen by Jesus, plus, according to many branches of Christianity, Paul.

Armageddon
In Christianity, the site where the final battle between good and evil will take place, during the Apocalypse.

Ascetics
People who deny themselves ordinary comforts in order to further their spiritual development, for example monks and nuns.

Atonement
In Judaism and Christianity, reconciliation or "at-oneness" with God. Usually thought to be achieved by making amends for sins.

Black Stone
A meteorite, now set into one corner of the Ka'bah in Mecca, and often kissed by Muslim pilgrims. It is traditionally believed to have been given to Ibrahim by Jibril.

Celtic religion
The faith practiced in pre-Roman times by the Celtic people of the western British Isles (especially Wales and Ireland) and in Brittany, France.

Chapel
A place set aside for prayer; the building used for worship by Nonconformist Christians.

Church
The building used for worship by Catholic, Orthodox, Anglican and some other Christian groups. The term also refers to Christians themselves, who together make up "the Church".

Circumcision
The cutting away of the foreskin of a boy's penis. This is a rite performed by Jews and Muslims in particular. The reason usually given is that it is one of God's laws.

Clergy
Officials of the Christian Church.

Confession
In Christianity, the formal admission of wrongdoings to a priest. The priest then gives the person absolution and generally suggests a small penance (punishment).

Coptic Church
A branch of Christianity which believes in the oneness of God, and not in the Trinity. It is found mainly in Egypt, but also in Ethiopia, Armenia and Syria.

Creed
A formal statement of belief, often repeated during religious rituals.

Cremation
The practice of burning corpses, rather than burying them. Some religions regard cremation as more in keeping with purity laws. Hindus, Buddhists and Sikhs cremate their dead.

Devout
Describes someone who is dedicated to their religion and follows its teachings devotedly.

Divine
Refers to God or a god; sacred, holy.

Doctrine
Teachings about beliefs.

Dreamtime
For Australian Aborigines, the time when their ancestors were thought to have roamed the world, creating everything in it.

Druids
The holy men of the Celtic religion.

Ecclesiastical
Refers to the Christian clergy and Church organization.

Ecumenism
A movement which aims for the unity of all Christians worldwide.

Eternity
Infinite time, without a beginning or an end; timelessness.

Ethics
The theories of how people should behave.

Evil
Wickedness, sin; the opposite of good.

Fatwa
A decision on a point of Islamic law made by a Muslim lawyer.

Ghat
In India, a flight of steps leading down to a sacred river. A "burning ghat" is the place at the top of the steps where Hindu cremations are held.

Grace
The love and help freely given by God to humanity, whether in the form of salvation or simply the answering of prayer; a prayer of thanksgiving for a meal.

Guru
A religious teacher, especially in Hinduism and Sikhism.

Halo
In works of art, a circle of light behind or above the head of a god or holy person.

Hell
A place or state of suffering for those who have done wrong.

Heresy
An opinion or teaching which contradicts the official, accepted teaching of a religion.

Hymn
A religious song.

Icon
In the Orthodox Church, a picture, often painted on wood, of Jesus, Mary or the saints, and believed to be sacred.

Idol
A picture or statue believed to contain spiritual power. People sometimes criticize members of other faiths as "idolaters", implying that they worship the idols themselves, rather than believing in an abstract God.

Incarnation
The embodiment of a god, or soul, in physical form. Jesus is seen as the incarnation of the Christian God.

Infidel
An unbeliever.

INRI
The Latin abbreviation for "Jesus of Nazareth, King of the Jews", which was nailed by the Romans to the cross on which Jesus was crucified.

Liberation theology
The theory that any kind of oppression (political, social or economic) is anti-Christian, as people are all equal in the sight of God. It originated in South America.

Madonna
Mary, the mother of Jesus.

Martyr
Someone who is killed or put through great suffering for their beliefs.

Millenarians
People who believe that when Christ comes again, he will rule on earth for a thousand years.

Monotheism
Belief in one God.

Morality
The code used to decide whether a course of action is right or wrong.

Mufti
A Muslim lawyer.

Mullah
A respected Muslim teacher or lawyer.

Mysticism
The quest for union with God or the spiritual by means of contemplation and meditation, for example.

Myth
A story which uses symbols to explore ideas about mysteries such as the origin of the world.

New Age religions
Recently established faiths which hope for a new age in which there will be peace and harmony. They tend to take their beliefs from very ancient sources and are often interested in the environment, psychotherapy and human potential.

Order
A society of monks or nuns living under the same religious rules and discipline.

Pantheism
The belief that the universe and the whole of nature are divine or sacred.

Polytheism
Belief in many gods.

Preach
Proclaim the beliefs, including the morality, of a religion.

Prophet
Someone said to have been chosen by God to speak out and reveal God's will to the world.

Puja
Hindu worship.

Purgatory
In Catholic and Orthodox Christianity, a place or state in which the souls of the dead prepare for heaven by making amends for their sins.

Purity
Spiritual and/or physical cleanliness. Rituals are often performed to achieve purity before worship, for example washing or confessing sins.

Redemption
Salvation from the consequences of wrongdoings. Christians believe that sin is wiped out through Jesus' death and resurrection.

Relic
A part of the body, clothing or belongings of a dead holy person.

Rite
A ritual.

Sacrament
An important Christian ceremony, such as the Eucharist or baptism.

Sacred thread ceremony
A ceremony for certain Hindu boys, indicating that they have reached adulthood for religious purposes. They are given a three-stranded thread, which they must always wear.

Sadhu
A Hindu holy person (usually male). Sadhus have left ordinary society to become ascetic.

Secular
Non-religious. Many societies are considered to be more secular than religious (Britain, for example).

Shema
A Jewish statement of faith which consists of three passages from the Torah and begins, "Hear, O Israel: the Lord is One." (Shema means "hear" in Hebrew.)

Shrine
A sacred building or place; a structure containing a sacred object.

Spirits
The souls of the dead; semi-powerful forces or beings thought to exist in nature.

Spiritualism
The belief that the living can communicate with the dead, especially through intermediaries known as mediums.

Temple
A building where worship takes place.

Theology
The study of God or the gods.

Transcendental meditation
A form of meditation, related to Hindu meditation, which is popular in the West. Many people practice it to reduce stress.

Transmigration of souls
The passage of the soul into another body after death; reincarnation, rebirth.

Transubstantiation
The belief, mainly in the Catholic Church, that the bread and wine of the Eucharist are transformed so that Christ is actually present in them. The priest is said to be the channel for this transformation but how it occurs is a mystery.

Vicar
Priest in the Anglican Church.

INDEX